Grow Your MONEY
Protect Your WEALTH

Grow Your MONEY
Protect Your WEALTH

Matthew Mellett, MS, CLU, ChFC

LUMINARE PRESS
WWW.LUMINAREPRESS.COM

LIMIT OF LIABILITY / DISCLOSURE OF WARRANTY

This book provides the opinion of the author and is for information purposes only. The information provided is subjective and may not apply to the reader's situation. Although the book is designed to provide accurate and authoritative information, the author and publisher provide no guarantees or warranties of any kind, expressed or implied, including but not limited to warranties of merchantability or fitness for a particular purpose. The book is sold with the understanding that the author and publisher are not engaged in providing legal, accounting, investment planning, or other professional advice; if such advice is required, the reader should seek the services of a competent professional. The author and publisher cannot be held liable for any loss of profit or other commercial damages resulting from the use of this book.

Grow Your Money Protect Your Wealth
Copyright © 2024 by Matthew Mellett, MS, CLU, ChFC

All rights reserved. This book or any portion thereof may not be reproduced or used in any manner whatsoever without the express written permission of the publisher, except for the use of brief quotations in a book review.

Printed in the United States of America

Luminare Press
442 Charnelton St.
Eugene, OR 97401
www.luminarepress.com

LCCN: 2024917128
ISBN: 979-8-88679-668-1

*for the benefit of all starting on
life's financial journey*

TABLE OF CONTENTS

Acknowledgment ix

Introduction 1

PART ONE
A Primer on Investing with Index Mutual Funds

1. The ABCs of Index Mutual Funds 7
2. Core Index Mutual Funds 18
3. How Do Index Mutual Funds
   Grow Your Money? 23
4. Capital Gains Distributions
   Generated by Index Mutual Funds 27
5. Financial Risks with Index Mutual Funds .. 31
6. The Power of Diversification to Manage
   Risks and Maximize Returns 36

PART TWO
Build Your Long-term Investment Portfolio

7. Determine Your Risk Profile 47
8. Select Your Asset Allocation 53
9. Choose Your Index Mutual Funds 56
10. Dollar Cost Average 68
11. Establish a Cost Basis Methodology 72
12. Rebalance 79
13. Tax-Advantaged Personal Investment Plans . 83
14. Seek Assistance from a
    Fee-Only Financial Planner 86

PART THREE
Case Studies

15. Case Study: Rachel,
    a 28-Year-Old Physical Therapist 91
16. Case Study: Alex,
    a 25-Year-Old Computer Programmer 100
17. Case Study: Tyler, a 35-Year-Old Engineer,
    and Claire, a 34-Year-Old English Teacher 109

PART FOUR
Protect Your Wealth

18. Establish an Emergency Fund 121
19. Insure against Financial Risks 124
20. Important and Necessary Documents 133
21. Perform an Annual Checkup 137

Conclusion 139

Notes 141

Acknowledgment

I would like to thank my parents for instilling in me good money habits and an appreciation for the importance of a good education.

Introduction

You worked hard. You studied hard. You applied yourself. You set a goal for yourself, and you achieved it. Perhaps you went to a trade school, joined the armed forces, or attended college or graduate school. You might have become an electrician, a plumber, a school teacher, a scientist, a computer programmer, or an engineer. Perhaps you are a nurse or a doctor.

Now that the preparation is over and you have achieved your goal of having a good job in a career you enjoy, you are likely living a comfortable and sensible life. You are earning a good income and not living beyond your means. Life is good, and you have found you have the extra income you believe you should be using to prepare yourself for the retirement years that will be here before you know it.

Grow Your Money Protect Your Wealth is written for people like yourself. In this book, I step you through a plan to invest your discretionary income in an efficient, cost-effective way. Discretionary income is the amount of money you have left for saving, investing, and spending on luxury items, such as vacations and nonessentials, after paying your taxes and personal necessities, such as food, clothing, and shelter. My plan will enable you to dramatically grow your discretionary income and lay the foundation for you to have a financially solid retirement.

In *Grow Your Money Protect Your Wealth*, I promote the use of index mutual funds as the investment vehicle of choice. Although there are other vehicles, such as actively managed mutual funds, exchange-traded funds, and individual stocks and bonds, I believe index mutual funds are the most cost-efficient and productive investment vehicle for investors like you to grow your money.

I am a firm believer in index mutual funds because I know investment markets are extremely efficient. Because they are so efficient, I believe it is very hard for even seasoned investment professionals, and most certainly novice investors, to outdo the market continuously through market timing. Market timers think they can buy and sell just the right security at just the right time and make a profit time and time again. When an investor market times, be they a professional or novice investor, they not only have to buy the right security at the right time, but they also have to sell that same security at the right time. Then they need to repeat the process over, and over, and over again. Through both academic study and real-world experiences, including interactions with other investors, I have learned that market timing is not a winning formula. I firmly believe it is a loser's game. You should as well.

In *Grow Your Money Protect Your Wealth*, I recommend a steady-eddy approach to investing. It may not be a flashy way to invest, and it will not provide you with spectacular stories of killings you made in the market to share with others. My plan will, however, allow you to succeed over the long haul and achieve the financial security you deserve in your retirement years.

As you grow your money and begin to accumulate wealth it is important that you protect yourself against the multitudes of financial risks. It is important to ensure hazards in life don't steal the wealth that you have worked hard to achieve. In Part Four of *Grow Your Money Protect*

Your Wealth, I describe the insurance products, important documents, and steps you need to take to protect yourself from these financial risks.

You have worked hard to reach the point of achieving the income you are making today. Grow your money and protect your wealth. You deserve no less.

—Matthew Mellett, MS, CLU, ChFC

*"If you would be wealthy,
think of saving,
as well as getting."*

—Benjamin Franklin

PART ONE

A Primer on Investing with Index Mutual Funds

CHAPTER ONE

The ABCs of Index Mutual Funds

A mutual fund can be thought of as a basket of financial assets. When you invest in a mutual fund, you pool your money with that of other investors to purchase a very broad range of financial assets. The two primary asset types you will buy are stocks and bonds.

A Little Background on Stocks

Stocks represent an ownership interest in a corporation. Corporations issue stock to obtain money with which to support and grow their business. After a company issues stock, investors buy and sell shares of that stock on the open market. When you purchase a share of stock, you become a shareholder, and you own equity in the corporation. A share of stock does not have a maturity date, and once you invest, there is no guarantee you will get any of your investment returned to you. There are two types of stock, common stock and preferred stock.

When you own common stock, you have an ownership interest in the company, which gives you the right to vote on major company issues, including the right to vote for the board of directors, which ensures the company's management serves the interest of the shareholders. You may also get to vote on whether or not the company should issue more stock or be sold to an outside buyer. As an owner of common stock, you may receive dividends, and you may see appreciation in the value of the shares. There is no guarantee, however, that you will, and there is a very real risk that you may see a decrease in the value of your shares. If the company goes bankrupt, your shares may very well become worthless.

The second type of stock is preferred stock. Like common stock, preferred stock represents ownership in a corporation. However, preferred stock is considered less risky than common stock as the preferred stock dividend is guaranteed and is paid before the dividend on shares of common stock. If the company becomes bankrupt, owners of preferred stock have a better chance than owners of common stock of getting some of their investment back. The downside of preferred stock is that the dividend is not increased in the event of greater company profits, and the share price does not increase in value as quickly as shares of common stock.

The reason a person buys shares of stock in a company is to make money, and there are two ways of doing so. The first is to receive dividend income from the shares of the stock. The second way is to benefit from capital appreciation as the price per share increases in value.

A company issues dividends as a means of sharing its earnings among shareholders. A company can choose not to pay a dividend and, instead, use earnings to grow the company. A young company just starting in a growth industry will likely not pay a dividend but rather use its earnings to purchase additional machinery or technology to grow the company. More mature companies, which may not have the growth potential of younger companies, will be more likely to issue dividends.

The price of a share of stock in a company is dependent on what people are willing to pay for it, which is dependent on the earnings of the company. If a company is doing well, is well-managed, and is selling large amounts of product at high profit margins, its success will be reflected in higher earnings per share. The more successful a company is, the more agreeable investors will be to pay for a share of those earnings. The more profitable a company becomes, the more investors will be willing to buy shares and the less inclined current shareholders will be to sell their shares. The supply and demand for shares of a company's stock will drive its price, and there is no limit to how high the shares of a company stock can go.

A Little Background on Bonds

Bonds are debt securities issued by governments and corporations. Bonds offer investors income in the form of fixed-interest payments. An investor in bonds will provide money to the issuer of the bond. In return, the issuer will provide the investor with regular interest payments, also known as coupon payments. A bond's face value, known as its par value, will be repaid upon the maturity of the bond. For example, an investor can purchase a 10-year bond with a par value of $1,000 and a coupon rate of 4%. In return, the investor will be paid $40 per year for 10 years. At the end of 10 years, the investor will receive the $1,000 face value of the bond in return.

There are many different types of bonds. The U.S. Treasury issues treasury bonds that are fully backed by the

U.S. government and do not have any default risk. Federal agency bonds are issued by federal agencies, such as the Government National Mortgage Association. Bonds issued by the Government National Mortgage Association are mortgage-backed securities and are fully guaranteed by the U.S. government. Other federal agency bonds are not fully guaranteed but have little risk of default.

Municipal bonds are issued by state and local governments and agencies. Their coupon payments are paid from the proceeds received from tax revenues and municipal projects, such as bridges or parks. Municipal bonds are classified into two categories: investment-grade and high-yield. Bonds issued by municipalities with strong balance sheets fall into the category of investment-grade while bonds issued by municipalities with a much greater chance of default are categorized as high-yield. As their name implies, high-yield municipal bonds will pay a higher rate of interest due to the greater risk the municipality will default on its interest payments.

Another type of bond is the corporate bond issued by corporations. Like municipal bonds, corporate bonds are classified into investment-grade and high-yield. Bonds issued by corporations with strong balance sheets fall into the category of investment-grade, while bonds issued by companies with a much greater chance of default are categorized as high-yield. Like their municipal bond counterparts, high-yield corporate bonds will pay a higher rate of interest due to the greater risk the company will default on its interest payments.

In addition to domestic bonds, there are foreign bonds. These bonds are issued by non-U.S. governments and corporations. Foreign bonds generally pay a higher rate of interest than domestic bonds due to a greater risk the foreign government or corporation will default on its interest payments.

Bonds also come with different maturities. There are short-term bonds with maturities from one to less than five years, intermediate-term bonds with maturities from five to ten years, and long-term maturities of more than 10 years.

The Benefits of Mutual Funds

There are many advantages to investing with mutual funds. Like an investment in an individual stock or bond, an investment in a mutual fund will allow you to benefit from the capital appreciation and/or income that the stock or bond will provide. A mutual fund, however, enables you to easily and inexpensively invest in a large number of stocks and/or bonds that would be difficult and costly for you to invest in on your own. By enabling you to invest in such a large number of assets, a mutual fund provides you with instant diversification. With such diversification, you greatly reduce the negative impact on your investment from the poor performance of a single stock or bond.

A second advantage of investing in mutual funds is that it allows you to invest in a large number of stocks and/or bonds with a very low minimum investment. Many mutual funds only require initial investments of $500, $1,000, or $3,000. Once invested in a mutual fund, you can make additional investments in the fund for as little as $25.

Last, mutual funds, which are sold by mutual fund families such as The Vanguard Group, Inc. or Fidelity Investments, are professionally managed by people who are very well-educated in the field of investments. Most mutual fund managers will possess the chartered financial analyst (CFA) designation or will have earned a master of business administration (MBA) degree with a concentration in financial analysis. They often will have years of experience in managing the mutual fund.

Types of Mutual Funds

The money you invest in a mutual fund will purchase shares of the fund, similar to purchasing shares of an individual stock. There are two broad types of mutual funds. The first is called an open-end mutual fund, and the second is a closed-end mutual fund.

With an open-end mutual fund, you buy and sell shares of the fund at a price based on the net asset value of the mutual fund. The net asset value is simply the market value of the stocks and bonds owned by the mutual fund plus any dividend or interest it may be owed, less any expenses, such as management fees, the mutual fund may owe. The net asset value is determined at the close of trading each day and is used to determine the share price of the mutual fund. The mutual fund share price, often quoted as the NAV, is the net asset value of the mutual fund divided by the number of shares owned by shareholders. For example, if a mutual fund owns shares of stock worth $50,075,000, including dividend and interest credits it may be owed, and owes $75,000 in management fees, the mutual fund will have a net asset value of [$50,075,000 - $75,000] or $50,000,000. If the mutual fund has 1,000,000 shares owned by shareholders, the mutual fund's share price will be [$50,000,000 / 1,000,000 shares] or $50 per share. If you invest $1,000 in the mutual fund, you will purchase [$1,000 / $50 per share] or 20 shares of the mutual fund.

A closed-end mutual fund is different from an open-end mutual fund in that a closed-end mutual fund issues shares to investors only when the mutual fund is first created. A closed-end mutual fund will not repurchase the shares directly from the investor like an open-end mutual fund. After the initial issue of a closed-end mutual fund, shares in the fund are bought and sold on stock exchanges. Because they are bought and sold this way, the price of the closed-end mutual fund is not based on the fund's net asset value, but rather on whatever the market supply and demand sets as a price for its shares. Therefore, closed-end mutual funds will often sell at a share price that is less than or more than what their net asset value would indicate. If a closed-end mutual fund sells for more, it is said to sell at a premium. If it sells for less, it is said to sell at a discount.

Fees Associated with Mutual Funds

There are many different types of fees associated with mutual funds. Some mutual funds have more types of fees than others. The size of the fees can vary widely as well.

The first type of fee is the load. A load can be a front-end load, assessed at the time of the investment, or it can be a back-end load that is assessed at the time of redemption when the shares of the mutual fund are sold. Mutual funds sold directly to investors will not typically assess a load. These types of mutual funds are referred to as "no-load" mutual funds. There are many mutual funds, however, sold to the public through brokers that will charge a load. The load will represent the fee paid to the broker for selling shares of the mutual fund. Loads, be they front-end or back-end, can vary dramatically. Historically, mutual funds that charge a load have not performed any better than mutual funds sold directly to investors without a load.

Another type of fee is the 12b-1 fee which is an annual marketing and distribution fee charged by some mutual funds. It is another fee that will eat away at your investment returns and do nothing to improve them.

A mutual fund may also assess a management fee. The management fee is charged to cover the salaries of the mutual fund manager and investment analysts. A high management fee does not guarantee a better management team. In addition, a mutual fund may charge an account maintenance fee to cover administrative costs associated with the mutual fund. A custodian fee can also be charged to cover payments to the custodian of the mutual fund. All of these fees can add up and reduce the actual return on your investment.

Managing a mutual fund does cost money, and the administrative fees, legal fees, and investment management expenses associated with managing a mutual fund must be borne by the shareholders. Some mutual funds are much better at controlling their costs than others, however. The best way to assess how efficiently a mutual fund is managed is to evaluate the fund's expense ratio, which reflects, as a percentage of the mutual fund's assets, the cost of all operating expenses, including management fees and 12b-1 fees but not loads. Some mutual funds will have expense ratios as low as 0.1% of mutual fund assets. Others will have expense ratios as high as 3%. The average expense ratio is approximately 1.5%. A difference of a fraction of a percent in expense ratio can make a dramatic difference in the ultimate returns achieved by an investor. Historically, and a bit ironically, mutual funds with lower expense ratios have tended to outperform those mutual funds with higher expense ratios.

Styles of Mutual Fund Management

There are two primary styles of mutual fund management, active and index. Mutual funds that are actively managed try to beat the market by providing a higher rate of return than the market average. Actively managed funds typically charge higher expenses to compensate for the additional research fees they incur. Actively managed funds typically do more buying and selling of financial assets and, thus, incur higher transaction costs, which are passed on to investors. Furthermore, more frequent transactions can result in greater capital gains distribution and taxes, as well. The expense ratio of the typical actively managed mutual fund is in the range of 1% to 3%.

An index-managed mutual fund, known simply as an index mutual fund, on the other hand, is designed to duplicate the rate of return of the market or a segment of the market. For example, an index mutual fund may duplicate the Wilshire 5000, which represents the entire U.S. stock market, or it may duplicate the S&P 500 and invest in the stock of 500 of the largest U.S. companies. Because an index mutual fund will mimic the market or a segment of the market, it does not incur expenses for researching financial assets. Index mutual funds also do not vary their portfolio of investments very often and, therefore, incur low transaction costs. Because there are few transactions, an index mutual fund will not generate large capital gains, resulting in lower capital gains taxes for the investor. Expense ratios of index mutual funds are much lower than those of their actively managed counterparts. The typical expense ratio of an index mutual fund is only in the 0.1% to 0.3% range.

Historically, index mutual funds have outperformed actively managed mutual funds. There are two reasons for this. First, as discussed, index mutual funds incur much lower expenses than actively managed mutual funds, and second, it is difficult for actively managed mutual funds to beat the market.

The lower expenses incurred by index mutual funds mean a greater portion of their investment returns is passed on to the investor. Over time, these lower expenses can result in a much higher rate of return. For example, all else being equal assume $10,000 is invested in two mutual funds each of which earns a rate of return of 8% per year for 20 years. Assume one fund is actively managed and has an expense ratio of 2%. Assume the other fund is an index mutual fund with an expense ratio of 0.2%. After 20 years, the actively managed mutual fund will accumulate to $32,071. The index mutual fund, however, will accumulate to $44,913. Because of the lower expense ratio, the index mutual fund accumulates an additional $12,842 or 40% more. Expense ratios make a huge difference over time and should not be ignored.

Expense ratios alone, however, are not the only reason why index mutual funds typically outperform actively managed mutual funds. The other reason is that it is very difficult to beat the market. Financial markets are extremely efficient. When an event occurs that will impact the market as a whole or an individual stock or bond, the financial markets are aware instantly and react accordingly. It is very hard to be ahead of the news and buy or sell ahead of others. In addition, when actively buying and selling in an attempt to beat the market, the active mutual fund manager must do so again and again and do so without error. Not only do they have to buy at the right time, but they must also sell at the right time, and then they must repeat the process over and over and over again. Actively buying and selling stocks has been called a loser's game, because it is just that, a no-win proposition.

Of course, there are actively managed mutual funds that will beat the market in a given year. But it is very rare for any one actively managed mutual fund to beat the market year after year. History has shown there to be an extremely low percentage of actively managed mutual funds that outperform the comparable index mutual fund time and time again. Be smart; choose index mutual funds over actively managed mutual funds as your investment vehicle of choice.

CHAPTER TWO

Core Index Mutual Funds

There are many different index mutual funds in which you can invest. As discussed in the previous chapter, index mutual funds include the two primary asset classes of stocks and bonds. Within each asset class, there are many from which to choose.

Stock index mutual funds will track U.S. and foreign stock, large-company stock, mid-size company stock, and small-company stock. These are often further broken down by investment styles, such as growth (stock in companies that are expected to have strong growth potential) or value (stock in companies whose stock is considered underpriced and of good value). Some stock index mutual funds track a specific industry sector, such as healthcare or technology.

There are also many different types of bond index mutual funds. Funds can invest in numerous types of bonds, including U.S. Treasury bonds, federal agency bonds, state and local municipal bonds, and corporate bonds. Some bond index mutual funds invest in investment-grade bonds while others invest in high-yield bonds. For each of these bond funds, there are three types of maturity: short-term, intermediate-term, and long-term.

Do not let yourself be overwhelmed by the great number of index mutual funds available. When you invest for the long term, you can grow your money with only a handful of funds selected from a group of core index mutual funds.

Following is a summary of core index mutual funds by asset class from which a well-rounded, long-term investment portfolio can be created. These core index mutual funds are open-end funds and are value-weighted based on the market values of the stocks and bonds in the index relative to the entire market value of the index. Value-weighted indexes give greater importance to the stocks and bonds with the greatest market value and are considered the true measure of a given stock or bond market. Actively managed mutual funds are measured against these core index mutual funds. You can grow your money and accumulate great wealth with them.

Stock Index Mutual Funds

The following are seven core stock index mutual funds from which a well-rounded, long-term investment portfolio can be created:

- **U.S. S&P 500 Stock Index** – The U.S. S&P 500 stock index mutual fund invests in 500 of the largest U.S. corporations across a broad mix of industrial companies, transportation companies, financial companies, and utilities. The companies in the U.S. S&P 500 stock index are chosen based on their size and industry. It is considered by many to be a representation and benchmark for the entire U.S. stock market.

- **U.S. Mid-Capitalization Stock Index** – The U.S. mid-capitalization stock index mutual fund invests in a broad mix of medium-sized U.S. corporations across all types of industries. The companies in the U.S. mid-capitalization stock index are smaller than those companies found in the U.S. S&P 500 stock index. Companies in the U.S. mid-capitalization stock index generally have a market capitalization between $2 billion and $10 billion.

- **U.S. Small-Capitalization Stock Index** – The U.S. small-capitalization stock index mutual fund invests in a broad mix of small-sized U.S. corporations across all types of industries. The companies in the U.S. small-capitalization stock index are smaller than those found in the U.S. S&P 500 stock index and U.S. mid-capitalization stock index. Companies in the U.S. small-capitalization stock index generally have a market capitalization between $300 million and $2 billion.

- **U.S. Total Stock Index** – The U.S. total stock index mutual fund invests in a broad mix of large, medium, and small companies across all types of industries and represents the entire U.S. stock market.

- **Foreign Developed Market Stock Index** – The foreign developed market stock index mutual fund invests in a broad mix of companies located in Europe, Asia, and Australia where there are high levels of economic security, growth, and industrialization.

- **Foreign Emerging Market Stock Index** – The foreign emerging market stock index mutual fund invests in a broad mix of companies located in countries with developing economies, such as Brazil, Russia, India, China, Thailand, Turkey, Mexico, Poland, and Malaysia. Emerging market economies tend to be less stable than those found in developed markets.

- **Foreign Total Stock Index** – The foreign total stock index mutual fund invests in a broad mix of companies located in developed and emerging markets around the world.

Bond Index Mutual Funds

The following are five core bond index mutual funds from which a well-rounded, long-term investment portfolio can be created:

- **U.S. Short-Term Bond Index** – The U.S. short-term bond index mutual fund invests in a broad mix of U.S. government and investment-grade corporate bonds with an average maturity from one to less than five years.

- **U.S. Intermediate-Term Bond Index** – The U.S. intermediate-term bond index mutual fund invests in a broad mix of U.S. government and investment-grade corporate bonds with an average maturity from five to 10 years.

- **U.S. Long-Term Bond Index** – The U.S. long-term bond index mutual fund invests in a broad mix of U.S. government and investment-grade corporate bonds with an average maturity of more than 10 years.

- **U.S. Total Bond Index** – The U.S. total bond index mutual fund invests in a broad mix of U.S. government and investment-grade corporate bonds that include short-term, intermediate-term, and long-term maturities.

- **Foreign Total Bond Index** – The foreign total bond index mutual fund invests in a broad mix of non-U.S. government and investment-grade corporate bonds issued from developed economies, such as Europe, Australia, and Japan, and from emerging market economies, such as Brazil, Russia, India, and China. The index includes bonds with short-term, intermediate-term, and long-term maturities.

CHAPTER THREE

How Do Index Mutual Funds Grow Your Money?

Wealth can be yours by investing for the long term in index mutual funds. These funds grow your money and create wealth in two ways: dividend income and the increase in the index mutual fund share price, otherwise known as capital appreciation.

Dividend Income

Many index mutual funds will receive dividends from the shares of stock and bonds they own. For example, shares of large-company stock owned by the index mutual fund often pay dividends. Bonds they hold will distribute interest payments. These income distributions received by the index mutual fund must then be distributed to the shareholders in the form of dividends. As a shareholder, you can choose to receive the dividend distribution in cash, or you can reinvest it by purchasing additional shares of the index mutual fund.

For example, assume you own 1,000 shares of an index mutual fund, and you receive a dividend distribution of

$500. You can use the $500 to purchase additional shares. If the fund has a share price of $10 per share, the $500 dividend distribution will purchase an additional [$500 / $10 per share] or 50 shares. The total number of shares you own will then be 1,050 shares.

Dividends received from an index mutual fund are taxed as ordinary income.

Capital Appreciation

As the market value of the stocks and bonds held by the index mutual fund increases, its share price will also increase in value. A higher share price will provide you with capital appreciation and increase the value of your investment.

For example, assume your index mutual fund owns shares of stock in 20 companies and has a net asset value of $1,000,000 with 100,000 shares outstanding to its investors. The share price will be [$1,000,000 / 100,000 shares] or $10 per share. If the rising market value of the stocks increases the net asset value to $1,200,000, the share price will increase to [$1,200,000 / 100,000 shares], or $12 per share.

If you originally invested $10,000 and purchased 1,000 shares of the index mutual fund, those shares would now be worth [1,000 shares x $12 per share] or $12,000. Had you also purchased 50 additional shares by reinvesting dividend income, as in the prior example, you would own 1,050 shares, and those shares would now be worth [1,050 shares x $12 per share] or $12,600. Through the reinvestment of dividend income and the power of capital appreciation, you would have seen your initial $10,000 investment grow to $12,600.

Time on Your Side

Although the share price of an index mutual fund will fluctuate over time, the trend over long periods will be upward. As an investor in an index mutual fund, you may experience 5% growth one year, followed by 25% growth the next, and then suffer a loss of 12% the year after that. Over long periods, however, you can expect to experience positive returns and an overall increase in the value of your index mutual fund.

As an example, let us look at a sample of historical values of the S&P 500 index.

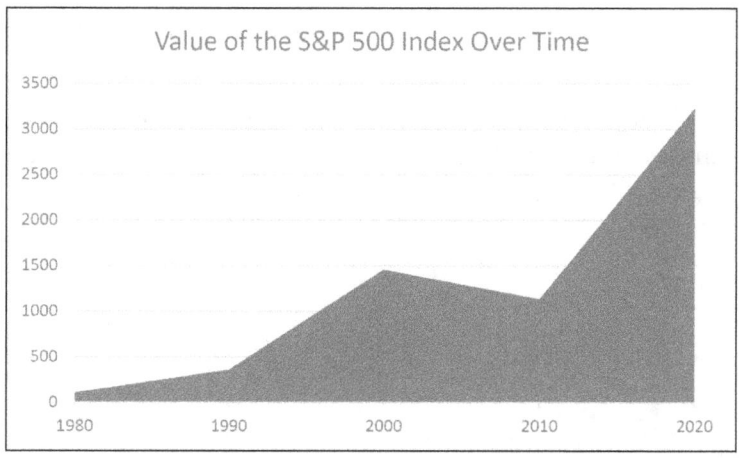

Figure 3-1 Value of the S&P 500 Index Over Time

As you can see in Figure 3-1, the value of the index increased dramatically over time. For the 40 years from 1980 to 2020, the index averaged an annual rate of return of 8.9%. You can also see that during shorter periods within those 40 years, the average annual rate of return varied significantly. For the 30 years from 1990 to 2020, it was 7.6%; from 2000 to 2020, it was 4.1%; and from 2010 to 2020, it was 11.1%. For the period from 1980 to 1990, the average annual rate of return was 13.0%; from 2000 to 2010, it was -2.5%. Though the returns came with great volatility, with both euphoric positive returns and wrenching negative returns, the overall trend over long periods is upward, providing positive average annual returns to investors.

Over time, an investment in an index mutual fund can tremendously grow your money. Assume you open an account with a mutual fund family and make an initial investment of $5,000 in an index mutual fund. If you continue to invest $1,000 per month in the fund over 40 years, and the fund earns an average annual return of 8.9% with a 0.1% expense ratio, your index mutual fund will grow to over $4.5 million. Not a bad chunk of change. Index mutual funds can indeed help you to grow your money and pave the way for you to live comfortably in retirement.

CHAPTER FOUR

Capital Gains Distributions Generated by Index Mutual Funds

In addition to dividend distributions, an index mutual fund will also generate capital gains distributions. When an index mutual fund sells shares of stock or sells a bond, it may sell the stock or bond for more than what it paid, thus earning a profit in the process. The profit from the sale of the stock or bond is a capital gain. The index mutual fund may also sell shares of stock or sell a bond for less than what it paid and take a loss. The loss from the sale of the stock or bond is a capital loss.

Capital losses realized by an index mutual fund are deducted from capital gains earned by the fund. If there are no capital gains in a given year, or if capital losses exceed capital gains, the fund will carry excess capital losses forward to be deducted against future capital gains. When capital gains exceed capital losses in a given year, however, capital gains distributions will be paid to the shareholders of the index mutual fund. This usually occurs at the end of the calendar year, though they can be distributed during the course of the year as well, depending upon the fund.

There are two types of capital gains realized by an index mutual fund: short-term and long-term. Short-term capital gains are earned on the sale of securities owned by the index mutual fund for one year or less. Like dividend distributions, short-term capital gains distributions are taxed to the shareholder at ordinary income tax rates. Long-term capital gains are earned on the sale of securities owned by the index mutual fund for more than one year. Long-term capital gains distributions are taxed to the shareholder at long-term capital gains tax rates which vary depending upon the shareholder's income tax bracket.

Capital gains realized by the index mutual fund are included in the net asset value of the fund. When the capital gains are distributed to the shareholders, the net asset value of the index mutual fund will be reduced by the amount of the distribution. As a result, the share price will also be reduced. Therefore, so as not to see the value of your index mutual fund decrease in value, it is important to reinvest all capital gains distributions back into the fund.

For example, assume your index mutual fund owns shares of stock in 20 companies and has a net asset value of $1,000,000 with 100,000 shares outstanding to its investors. The share price of the index mutual fund will be [$1,000,000 / 100,000 shares] or $10 per share. If the fund sells shares of stock resulting in a long-term capital gain of $100,000 in a calendar year, it will distribute a long-term capital gain of [$100,000 /100,000 shares] or $1 per share. The net asset value of the index mutual fund will be reduced to [$1,000,000 - $100,000] or $900,000. The share price will be reduced to [$900,000 / 100,000 shares] or $9 per share.

If you own 1,000 shares of the index mutual fund, you would have had an investment worth [1,000 shares x $10 per share] or $10,000 before the long-term capital gain distribution. After the long-term capital gain distribution, the 1,000 shares would only be worth [1,000 shares x $9 per share] or $9,000. Although the value of your index mutual fund has decreased in value as a result of the long-term capital gain distribution, you have not lost money as you now have a capital gain distribution of [1,000 shares x $1 per share] or $1,000. The shares of your index mutual fund, now worth $9,000, plus the $1,000 long-term capital gain distribution, sum to $10,000, the value of your index mutual fund before the long-term capital gain distribution.

To maintain the value of your index mutual fund, however, it is important to automatically reinvest all capital gains distributions, be they short-term or long-term. Continuing with the example, when the $1,000 long-term capital gain distribution is reinvested at a share price of $9 per share, [$1,000 / $9 per share] or 111.111 shares will be purchased. You will then own [1,000 shares + 111.111 shares] or 1,111.111 shares of the index mutual fund with a value of [1,111.111 x $9 per share] or $10,000, which is the value of your fund before the long-term capital gain distribution was made.

Unlike dividend distributions from stock dividends or bond interest payments, which help you to grow your money by adding value to your index mutual fund, capital gains distributions do not. Because you must pay tax on capital gains distributions, without the benefit of added value to your fund, they hinder your effort to accumulate wealth.

Capital gains distributions, therefore, are another reason to choose index mutual funds over actively managed mutual funds. Because actively managed mutual funds are trying to beat the market index, they typically do more buying and selling of the securities held by the fund, generating more capital gains distributions and a higher tax bill in the process. Index mutual funds, which are much more passive in their investment strategy, tend to have a much lower turnover rate than their actively managed counterparts. The more passive strategy results in far fewer sell transactions and subsequently fewer capital gains distributions and a smaller tax bill.

CHAPTER FIVE

Financial Risks with Index Mutual Funds

As everyone knows, without risk there is no reward. This adage applies to investments in index mutual funds, as well. Though investing in index mutual funds can help you grow your money and bring you great financial rewards over the long term, achieving those rewards requires that you take on financial risks.

The financial risks to which an investor is exposed will vary by the type of index mutual fund in which they invest. A bond index mutual fund will have different financial risks than a stock index mutual fund. A foreign index mutual fund will have financial risks that a domestic, U.S. index mutual fund will not. Following is a summary of the types of financial risks you may incur when investing in index mutual funds.

Risks Associated with Stock Index Mutual Funds

Stock index mutual funds use shareholder investments to purchase shares of company stock. When you purchase company stock, you become an owner of the company which allows you to share in the increased value of the company and the dividends it pays. An investment in a stock index mutual fund comes with the following financial risks:

- **Stock Market Risk** – Stock market risk is the risk that stock prices will decline. The stock market is cyclical. There are periods when it is rising and periods when it is falling in value. At times, price swings in the stock market can be extremely volatile. An investment in any stock index mutual fund is subject to stock market risk.

- **Investment Style Risk** – Investment style risk is the risk that a certain segment of the market is out of favor and exhibits a decline in the value of the stock. For example, suppose that during investment cycles, small companies may be considered in favor by the investment community. As investors move their money into small-company stock, they may move their investment dollars out of large-company stock. Also, companies are categorized as growth companies or value companies. A growth company is one that investors believe will exhibit tremendous growth in revenues and profits. A value company is one that investors think is currently undervalued and is a good value for the price. At times, the investor community may favor growth stocks over value stocks and vice versa. Investment style risk is the risk then that the stocks in which you are invested are currently out of favor and, thus, decline in value as a result.

Investments in the U.S. S&P 500 stock index, U.S. mid-capitalization stock index, and the U.S. small-capitalization stock index are all subject to stock market and investment style risks. Historically, the U.S. mid-capitalization and the

U.S. small-capitalization stock indexes have been subject to greater financial risks than the U.S. S&P 500 stock index.

Risks Associated with Bond Index Mutual Funds

Bond index mutual funds use shareholder investments to purchase bonds. A bond is an IOU (I owe you). When you purchase a bond, you are giving money to someone with the promise they will pay you interest on the IOU over a specified period and return your principal by or at the end of the specified period, also known as the maturity date. An investment in a bond index mutual fund comes with the following financial risks:

- **Interest Rate Risk** – Interest rate risk is the risk that the price of a bond index mutual fund will decline as interest rates rise. When interest rates rise, a bond becomes less valuable because the interest rate it is paying is less than the interest rate offered by a newly issued bond. If a bond index mutual fund owns a bond that is paying 3% interest but rates rise to 4%, the bond paying 3% becomes less valuable. The decrease in the value of the bond will result in a decrease in the net asset value of the bond index mutual fund. Bond index mutual funds that invest in long-term maturities have higher interest rate risk than those funds that invest in intermediate-term maturities which in turn will have higher interest rate risk than bond index mutual funds that invest in short-term maturities.

- **Income Risk** – Income risk is the risk that a bond index mutual fund will pay less income if interest rates decrease. If a bond paying 3% matures, the proceeds from the bond will be used to purchase a new bond. If interest rates have decreased to 2%, however, the income generated by the new bond will be less than what was previously being earned.

- **Default Risk** – Default risk, also known as credit risk, is the risk that the issuer of a bond fails to pay the interest or principal due as promised, or that the value of a bond falls if the financial community believes the issuer of the bond may not make payments on time. This type of risk is specific to the issuer and is generally very low in a bond index mutual fund that is diversified among many bond issuers.

Risks Associated with Foreign Index Mutual Funds

Foreign index mutual funds are funds that invest in stocks and bonds of non-U.S. companies and governments. A foreign stock index mutual fund will exhibit stock market risk and investment style risk just like a U.S. stock index mutual fund. A foreign bond index mutual fund will exhibit interest rate risk, income risk, and default risk just like a U.S. bond index mutual fund. In addition, however, foreign stock index mutual funds and foreign bond index mutual funds exhibit unique financial risks.

- **Country Risk** – Country risk is the risk that an event specific to a country, such as a natural disaster, a financial crisis, or political upheaval, will negatively impact the price of a foreign index mutual fund.

- **Currency Risk** – Currency risk is the risk that an investment in a foreign country will decline in value when measured in U.S. dollars due to unfavorable changes in currency exchange rates.

Yes, investments in index mutual funds come with several financial risks. These risks, however, should not deter you from investing in index mutual funds. As you will learn in the next chapter, these risks can be mitigated and managed so that you can capture the financial benefits of index mutual funds and still be able to sleep at night.

CHAPTER SIX

The Power of Diversification to Manage Risks and Maximize Returns

As learned in the previous chapter, many different financial risks arise as a result of investing in index mutual funds. There is stock market risk, investment style risk, interest rate risk, income risk, default risk, country risk, and currency risk. Financial risks differ between stock and bond index mutual funds and even vary from one bond index mutual fund to another and from one stock index mutual fund to another. But what exactly do these financial risks mean to your hard-earned dollars invested in an index mutual fund?

Financial risks equate to price volatility and the variance in the rate of return you will earn on your investment. For example, an investment in an index mutual fund may provide you with an average rate of return of 9% annually over 20 years, but that 9% average rate of return may come in the form of great volatility. You may earn 25%

one year but lose 15% the next. You could have three or four years in a row earning 20% or more and then lose 45% in the fifth year. In short, an investment in an index mutual fund can be a wild ride. The ups and downs in the net asset value of the fund and the corresponding investment returns are called volatility. The greater the volatility, the greater the financial risk associated with the index mutual fund. Another way to think about financial risk is to consider it to be the level of surprise associated with each year's rate of return.

When you take on greater financial risk and greater volatility, however, you can expect to be paid a benefit known as the risk premium. The risk premium will be paid to you in the form of higher average rates of return over a long-term investment period. Investment in stock index mutual funds comes with greater financial risk and greater volatility than an investment in bond index mutual funds. The reason for this is that investment in shares of stock is a bet on future corporate earnings, which are very uncertain and volatile. An investment in bonds is a bet a lender will pay you a promised rate of interest which, historically, is more reliable than a bet on a company's future earnings. Thus, as a reward for greater financial risk, stock index mutual funds will pay a higher average annual rate of return over a long-term investment period.

For example, an investment solely in a stock index mutual fund may provide a 9.5% average annual rate of return over 20 years, but over those 20 years, you may see a high annual rate of return of positive 50% as well as a low annual rate of return of negative 45%. An investment solely in a less risky, less volatile bond index mutual fund, however, may only provide a 5.5% average annual rate of return over 20 years. The bond index mutual fund, however, will have less volatile annual rates of return. Its high annual rate of return over the 20 years may be positive 30% and its low annual rate of return negative 8%. As in this example, stock index mutual funds tend to have a much wider range of returns than bond index mutual funds. So, though the stock index mutual fund provides a higher average annual rate of return of 9.5% or a 4% risk premium above the bond index mutual fund, the 9.5% rate of return comes with much greater volatility in the net asset value and each year's annual rate of return.

How do you, as an investor, maximize your average annual rate of return but manage the volatility, and the financial risk, to a level at which you are comfortable? The answer is through diversification of the asset classes, or the mix of stocks and bonds, in which you invest. Researchers have tracked the rates of returns on stocks and bonds for many, many years and a broad swath of investment periods. They have tracked returns through depressions and recessions, through economic boom times, periods of war, and periods of peace. The following table illustrates average, annual rates of return that an investor can reasonably target based on long-term, historical rates of returns. The targeted, average, annual rate of return varies as a function of the mix of stock index mutual funds and bond index mutual funds. In addition to the average annual rates of return, the table provides targeted, high, and low annual rates of return ranges to paint a picture of the type of volatility an investor could experience if invested in that mix of stock index mutual funds and bond index mutual funds.

% Stock Index Mutual Funds	% Bond Index Mutual Funds	Targeted Average Annual Rate of Return	Targeted High / Low Annual Rate of Return
100%	0%	9.5%	+50% / -45%
80%	20%	9.0%	+45% / -35%
60%	40%	8.5%	+35% / -30%
50%	50%	8.0%	+30% / -25%
40%	60%	7.5%	+25% / -20%
20%	80%	6.5%	+30% / -10%
0%	100%	5.5%	+30% / -8%

Table 6-1 Targeted Rates of Return by Mix of Stock Index Mutual Funds and Bond Index Mutual Funds

As you can see in Table 6-1, the average annual rates of return and the range of returns vary dramatically depending upon the mix of stock index mutual funds and bond index mutual funds. A 100% investment in stock index mutual funds has a targeted, average, annual rate of return of 9.5%, whereas a 100% investment in bond index mutual funds has a targeted, average, annual rate of return of just 5.5%. The difference of 4% annually can make a huge difference in the value of your investment over a long-term investment period. For example, if you invested $5,000 annually for 30 years and earned 9.5% annually on the investment, your investment would be worth $819,539. If you earned 5.5% annually, however, your investment would only be worth $382,097.

With such a huge gap in the earnings potential between stock index mutual funds and bond index mutual funds, one would think everyone would invest all of their money in stock funds and none at all in bond funds. Not so quick. As the table also points out, a 100% investment in stock index mutual funds comes with a very wide range of returns, including very large negative returns. Whereas, a 100% investment in bond index mutual funds comes with a targeted, low, annual rate of return of negative 8%, a 100% investment in stock index mutual funds comes with a targeted, low, annual rate of return of negative 45%.

What does this mean to you as an investor? Assume you invest $5,000 annually in stock index mutual funds. After 15 years of investing, your stock index mutual funds could potentially be worth $167,207 assuming an average annual rate of return of 9.5%. If due to a bad recession or catastrophic natural disaster, your stock index mutual fund can lose 45% of its value. Your $167,207 portfolio of stock index mutual funds can plummet in value to $91,964. The decrease in value can happen in a matter of weeks if not days. Such a large decrease in the value of an investment portfolio is something not everyone can handle emotionally.

On the other hand, assume you invest $5,000 annually in bond index mutual funds. After 15 years of investing, your bond index mutual funds could potentially be worth $118,205, assuming an average annual rate of return of 5.5%. Due to rising interest rates, however, your bond index mutual funds may lose 8% of their value. In this instance, your $118,205 portfolio of bond index mutual funds can decrease in value to $108,749. Such a smaller decrease in the value of an investment portfolio is much easier for some investors to accept.

For many people, the extreme gyrations associated with a 100% investment in stock index mutual funds are too wild a ride. On the other hand, a 100% investment in bond index mutual funds may not provide enough of an investment return.

By adjusting the mix between stock index mutual funds and bond index mutual funds, an investor can maximize their targeted, average, annual rate of return while maintaining an acceptable level of volatility.

Continuing the same example, assume you invest $5,000 annually in a portfolio of 40% stock index mutual funds and 60% bond index mutual funds. After 15 years of investing, your investment portfolio could potentially be worth $140,386, assuming an average annual rate of return of 7.5%. If due to economic conditions, such as a recession, your stock index mutual funds may plummet in value, but your bond index mutual funds may maintain their net asset values. As a result, your portfolio may fall just 20%, reducing your investment to $112,309. This level of volatility may be more acceptable to you as an investor while still providing you with a higher and more acceptable rate of return.

Why You Need to Take Risk and Maximize Your Return

You may be asking yourself why you need to take on additional financial risk with stock index mutual funds, rather than settle for a lower rate of return and the much lower level of volatility that comes with bond index mutual funds. The simple answer is inflation.

Inflation is the phenomenon by which the value of a dollar, or any other currency, lessens over time. Because of inflation, it requires more dollars to purchase an item, be it a bicycle, groceries, or a house, as time goes by. Because of inflation, a book that may cost $10 today will likely cost $12 five years from now. Inflation occurs when there is an abundance of dollars chasing too few products. When this happens, prices increase and the relative value of the dollar decreases. Inflation is measured as the annual percentage rate of increase in the price of products. It typically has averaged 3% to 4% annually.

Over a period of 30 years, the impact of inflation can be quite dramatic. If today you spend $400 per month on groceries and inflation averages 3% annually, those same groceries may cost you $970 per month in 30 years. If inflation averages 5% annually, those same groceries may cost you $1,728 per month, 30 years down the road. An easy rule of thumb to estimate the impact of inflation is the Rule of 72. If you divide 72 by the rate of inflation, you will find the number of years it will take for the price of a product to double in cost. For example, if inflation averages 3% annually, it will take 24 years for the price of a product to double in cost. If inflation averages 6% annually, however, it will only take 12 years for the price of a product to double. At a 3% rate of inflation, a new car that sells for $25,000 today will likely cost $50,820 in 24 years, about the time you may be looking to retire. And at a 6% rate of inflation, it will only take 12 years before the price of the car reaches that level.

Thus, because of inflation, you can expect the cost of living in your retirement years to be much higher than the cost of living in today's world. And though inflation historically has averaged 3% to 4% annually, there is no guarantee it will not be 5% or 7% or even higher. If you invest solely in bond index mutual funds which have a targeted, average, annual rate of return of 5.5%, you may not grow your investments enough to keep pace with inflation. For you to ensure you have the dollars you need in your retirement years to maintain a comfortable quality of life and afford the items you need and desire, it is important to take on financial risks and maximize the rate of return from your investments.

But Do Not Forget About Volatility

Keep in mind that though inflation and your desire to maintain a comfortable lifestyle will make you want to choose a mix of stock index mutual funds and bond index mutual funds with the highest, targeted, average, annual rate of return, you must be able to live with the corresponding level of volatility. It is extremely important to remember that the level of volatility increases with a greater percentage of stock index mutual funds in your portfolio. If you can tolerate the wild rides associated with a 100% investment in stock index mutual funds, then reach for the 9.5% average annual rate of return that you will likely receive. Be sure to know yourself, however. Many people think they can tolerate a dramatic drop in the value of their investment, but when it happens, they realize they cannot. In summary, choose the mix of stock index mutual funds and bond index mutual funds that provide the highest level of return with the greatest amount of volatility you can tolerate. Part Two of *Grow Your Money Protect Your Wealth* will help you to do just that.

PART TWO

Build Your Long-term Investment Portfolio

CHAPTER SEVEN

Determine Your Risk Profile

The first step in building your long-term investment portfolio with index mutual funds is to assess how much volatility in the value of your investments you can comfortably tolerate. Although only you can determine how much volatility, or risk, you can accept, the following questionnaire can assist you in thinking about your risk profile.

The Risk Assessment Questionnaire contains 15 questions that will help you assess your level of risk tolerance. The questions asked will assess your investment time horizon, the stability of your income, your propensity for saving and managing debt, and your level of comfort with change and volatility in your portfolio.

After completing the questionnaire, you will be given one to four points for each question depending on your answer. The total points you receive will indicate your ability to take on risk and be comfortable with volatility in your investment portfolio. Based on your total points, a risk profile of very aggressive, aggressive, moderate, conservative, or very conservative will be given to you.

Risk Assessment Questionnaire

Question #1: What is your age?

    A. 35 years or younger

    B. 36 to 54 years

    C. 55 to 64 years

    D. 65 years or older

Question #2: When do you expect to use the money you are now planning to invest?

    A. In more than 20 years

    B. In 11 to 20 years

    C. In 5 to 10 years

    D. In less than 5 years

Question #3: Over what length of time do you expect to spend the money once you begin to withdraw from the investment portfolio?

    A. More than 20 years

    B. 11 to 20 years

    C. 5 to 10 years

    D. Less than 5 years

Question #4: How would you describe your future income over the next several years?

    A. Very reliable

    B. Reliable

    C. Unreliable

    D. Very unreliable

Question #5: Do you have an emergency fund in place and for how long will it cover your expenses in the event of a job loss?

    A. Yes, more than 2 years
    B. Yes, 6 months to 2 years
    C. Yes, less than 6 months
    D. No, I do not have an emergency fund

Question #6: How would you describe your level of debt?

    A. I do not have debt
    B. I have a small amount of debt
    C. I have a fair amount of debt
    D. I have a significant amount of debt

Question #7: How would you describe your understanding of investments?

    A. Excellent
    B. Good
    C. Limited
    D. Extremely limited

Question #8: How many years of experience do you have with investment products?

    A. More than 20 years
    B. 11 to 20 years
    C. 5 to 10 years
    D. Less than 5 years

Question #9: In the past, when you have experienced a surprising change in your life that presented challenges, such as losing a job or being forced to relocate, were you:

A. Excited about a new opportunity
B. Concerned about the change, but able to manage the situation
C. Initially unhappy but eventually able to cope
D. Extremely unhappy and emotionally stressed

Question #10: If you are a contestant on a game show and have the choice of keeping $10,000 or winning more, which do you choose?

A. A 10% chance of winning $100,000
B. A 25% chance of winning $50,000
C. A 50% chance of winning $20,000
D. The $10,000

Question #11: Which investment portfolio would you choose?

A. Portfolio A: Earns either a 50% return or a 25% loss
B. Portfolio B: Earns either a 30% return or a 15% loss
C. Portfolio C: Earns either a 15% return or a 7% loss
D. Portfolio D: Earns either an 8% return or a 3% loss

Question #12: If your investment portfolio lost 30% of its value in two months, how long would you wait for your investment portfolio to regain its value before making changes to your allocations or contribution levels?

A. 2 years or more
B. More than 1 year but less than 2 years
C. 6 months to 1 year
D. Less than 6 months

Question #13: Which investment portfolio would you prefer?
- A. Portfolio A: 10% return with a high degree of volatility to principal
- B. Portfolio B: 7% return with a medium degree of volatility to principal
- C. Portfolio C: 5% return with a low degree of volatility to principal
- D. Portfolio D: 3% return with no volatility to principal

Question #14: If there were a severe economic crisis and the value of your investment portfolio decreased by 50%, what would you do?
- A. Leave the investment portfolio as is and continue making additional investments as planned
- B. Leave the investment portfolio as is but stop making additional investments
- C. Move a portion of the investment portfolio from more risky stock index mutual funds to less risky bond index mutual funds
- D. Move the investment portfolio into a federally insured, bank savings account

Question #15: What is the maximum loss in your investment portfolio with which you would be comfortable over a 6-month period?
- A. 40% to 50% decline
- B. 25% to 30% decline
- C. 10% to 15% decline
- D. 0% to 5% decline

Scoring Your Risk Assessment Questionnaire

To score your Risk Assessment Questionnaire, give yourself four points for every question you answered with A, three points for every question you answered with B, two points for every question you answered with C, and one point for every question you answered with D. Total your points and determine your risk profile as follows:

- **55 to 60 Points => Very Aggressive:**
  If your total score is 55 to 60 points, then you are an extremely strong risk-taker, and a very aggressive investment portfolio is likely best for you.

- **45 to 54 Points => Aggressive:**
  If your total score is 45 to 54 points, then you are a strong risk-taker, and an aggressive investment portfolio is appropriate for you.

- **33 to 44 Points => Moderate:**
  If your total score is 33 to 44 points, then you are a moderate risk-taker, and a moderate investment portfolio is appropriate for you.

- **21 to 32 Points => Conservative:**
  If your total score is 21 to 32 points, then you are a conservative risk-taker, and a conservative investment portfolio is appropriate for you.

- **15 to 20 Points => Very Conservative:**
  If your total score is 15 to 20 points, then you are a very conservative risk-taker, and a very conservative investment portfolio is appropriate for you.

CHAPTER EIGHT

Select Your Asset Allocation

Before you select specific index mutual funds in which to invest, it is important to first decide upon an asset allocation that is suitable for you as an investor. As we learned in Chapter Six, the asset allocation, or mix of stock index mutual funds and bond index mutual funds, can result in very different annual rates of return as well as wide ranges of volatility associated with those returns. We saw that a portfolio consisting of 100% stock index mutual funds may have a targeted, average, annual rate of return of 9.5% but be subject to returns that may be positive 50% in one year and negative 45% in another. On the other end of the spectrum, we saw that a portfolio consisting of 100% bond index mutual funds may provide a targeted, average, annual rate of return of 5.5% but provide returns in a more narrow, less volatile, range, varying from positive 30% to negative 8%. A study by Brinson, Hood, and Beebower titled, "Determinants of Portfolio Performance" and published in the *Financial Analysts Journal* in 1986, states that, on average, 93.6% of the variability associated with a portfolio's return is explained by its asset allocation.

In choosing an asset allocation, an investor needs to evaluate various asset allocations and the targeted, average, annual rates of return, and the targeted, annual rate of return ranges they likely will generate. As a long-term investor, you want to choose an asset allocation that will provide the highest rate of return with a level of volatility with which you are comfortable. The result of the Risk Assessment Questionnaire in Chapter Seven is an indicator of the level of risk you can tolerate. If the results of the questionnaire indicate you are a very aggressive investor, then an asset allocation consisting of more volatile stock index mutual funds is going to be more appropriate for you. If the results indicate you are a moderate investor, then an asset allocation consisting of a mix of stock index mutual funds and bond index mutual funds is going to be the right asset allocation for you.

Following are recommended asset allocation models for each of the risk profiles assessed in the Risk Assessment Questionnaire. For each asset allocation model, the targeted, average, annual rate of return and the targeted, high and low annual rate of return are shown. The targeted, high and low annual rate of return shown for each asset allocation conveys the level of volatility you might expect from the asset allocation model.

Use the results of the Risk Assessment Questionnaire you completed in Chapter Seven to select one of the asset allocation models in Table 8-1.

Asset Allocation Model	% Stock Index Mutual Funds	% Bond Index Mutual Funds	Targeted Average Annual Rate of Return	Targeted High / Low Annual Rate of Return
Model A – Very Aggressive	100%	0%	9.5%	+50% / -45%
Model B – Aggressive	80%	20%	9.0%	+45% / -35%
Model C – Moderate	60%	40%	8.5%	+35% / -30%
Model D – Conservative	40%	60%	7.5%	+25% / -20%
Model E – Very Conservative	20%	80%	6.5%	+30% / -10%

Table 8-1 Recommended Asset Allocation Models

So, for example, if the result of the Risk Assessment Questionnaire indicates you are a very aggressive investor, then you should choose Model A – Very Aggressive with an asset allocation consisting of 100% stock index mutual funds. If the result of the Risk Assessment Questionnaire indicates you are a conservative investor, then you should choose Model D – Conservative with an asset allocation of 40% stock index mutual funds and 60% bond index mutual funds. Again, be sure you are comfortable with the level of volatility associated with the asset allocation model you choose.

CHAPTER NINE

Choose Your Index Mutual Funds

Once you have decided upon an asset allocation that will maximize your annual rate of return while limiting volatility to a level at which you are comfortable, it is time to choose the actual index mutual funds in which you will invest.

As discussed in Chapter Two, and shown in Table 9-1, there are 12 core index mutual funds from which a sound investment portfolio can be built.

Stock Index Mutual Funds	Bond Index Mutual Funds
U.S. S&P 500 Stock Index	U.S. Short-term Bond Index
U.S. Mid-Cap Stock Index	U.S. Intermediate-term Bond Index
U.S. Small-Cap Stock Index	U.S. Long-term Bond Index
U.S. Total Stock Index	U.S. Total Bond Index
Foreign Developed Market Stock Index	Foreign Total Bond Index
Foreign Emerging Market Stock Index	
Foreign Total Stock Index	

Table 9-1 Core Index Mutual Funds

Following are sample portfolios using these core index mutual funds which you can choose to build your portfolio. You can use these portfolios as is, or you can modify them for your personal preferences. The portfolios are categorized according to the risk profiles from which you selected your asset allocation in Chapter Eight.

For each risk profile and asset allocation (very aggressive, aggressive, moderate, conservative, and very conservative), two investment portfolios are given. The first is labeled the Simple Portfolio Approach. The second is labeled the Focused Portfolio Approach. Each of these two portfolios is appropriate for the given risk profile, and each has the same asset allocation.

The Simple Portfolio Approach utilizes broad-based, index mutual funds, such as the U.S. Total Stock Index mutual fund, and keeps the number of funds in the portfolio to two to four funds. The Simple Portfolio Approach is better suited to investors who want to keep their finances less complex and who want to keep the number of index mutual funds they own and the corresponding administration of those funds to a minimum.

The Focused Portfolio Approach utilizes index mutual funds that are more targeted than those used in the Simple Portfolio Approach. For example, the Focused Portfolio Approach will utilize a combination of bond index mutual funds, such as the U.S. long-term, U.S. intermediate-term, and U.S. short-term bond index mutual funds, rather than using only the broad-based, U.S. total bond index mutual fund. The Focused Portfolio Approach will be better suited to those who would like to fine-tune their investment selections among different segments of the stock market and bond market.

Neither the Simple Portfolio Approach nor the Focused Portfolio Approach is better than the other. Both portfolio types will be in line with the risk profile you determined in Chapter Seven and the asset allocation you selected in Chapter Eight. If the amount of money you have available to begin an investment plan is limited, the Simple Portfolio Approach may be more practical for you. Index mutual funds have a minimum initial investment amount, and since the Simple Portfolio Approach utilizes a fewer number of funds than the Focused Portfolio Approach, it requires a smaller initial investment to implement. Choosing one portfolio approach, simple or focused, over the other is a matter of personal preference.

In addition to the index mutual funds comprising each portfolio, the targeted, average, annual rate of return and the targeted level of volatility are shown in the following sample portfolios. When selecting the portfolio in which you plan to invest, think again about the targeted, average, annual rate of return and the targeted level of volatility. It cannot be emphasized enough the importance of choosing a portfolio that maximizes your targeted, average, annual rate of return with a level of volatility with which you are comfortable.

- **PORTFOLIO TYPE #1** – A portfolio that consists of 100% stock index mutual funds for very aggressive, long-term investors.

    Simple Portfolio Approach:

    - 80% U.S. total stock index mutual fund

    - 20% foreign total stock index mutual fund

Focused Portfolio Approach:

- 30% U.S. S&P 500 stock index mutual fund
- 25% U.S. mid-capitalization stock index mutual fund
- 25% U.S. small-capitalization stock index mutual fund
- 10% foreign developed market stock index mutual fund
- 10% foreign emerging market stock index mutual fund

Targeted average annual rate of return: +9.5%.

Targeted level of volatility: Extremely high level of volatility with targeted high and low annual rates of return of +50% and -45%.

- **PORTFOLIO TYPE #2** – A portfolio that consists of 80% stock index mutual funds and 20% bond index mutual funds for aggressive, long-term investors.

Simple Portfolio Approach:

- 60% U.S. total stock index mutual fund
- 20% foreign total stock index mutual fund
- 10% U.S. total bond index mutual fund
- 10% foreign total bond index mutual fund

Focused Portfolio Approach:

- 30% U.S. S&P 500 stock index mutual fund
- 15% U.S. mid-capitalization stock index mutual fund

- 15% U.S. small-capitalization stock index mutual fund
- 10% foreign developed market stock index mutual fund
- 10% foreign emerging market stock index mutual fund
- 10% U.S total bond index mutual fund
- 10% foreign total bond index mutual fund

Targeted average annual rate of return: +9.0%.

Targeted level of volatility: Very high level of volatility with targeted high and low annual rates of return of +45% and -35%.

- **PORTFOLIO TYPE #3** – A portfolio that consists of 60% stock index mutual funds and 40% bond index mutual funds for moderate, long-term investors.

Simple Portfolio Approach:

- 40% U.S. total stock index mutual fund
- 20% foreign total stock index mutual fund
- 30% U.S. total bond index mutual fund
- 10% foreign total bond index mutual fund

Focused Portfolio Approach:

- 20% U.S. S&P 500 stock index mutual fund
- 10% U.S. mid-capitalization stock index mutual fund
- 10% U.S. small-capitalization stock index mutual fund

- 10% foreign developed market stock index mutual fund
- 10% foreign emerging market stock index mutual fund
- 10% U.S. long-term bond index mutual fund
- 10% U.S. intermediate-term bond index mutual fund
- 10% U.S. short-term bond index mutual fund
- 10% foreign total bond index mutual fund

Targeted average annual rate of return: +8.5%.

Targeted level of volatility: High level of volatility with targeted high and low annual rates of return of +35% and -30%.

- **PORTFOLIO TYPE #4** – A portfolio that consists of 40% stock index mutual funds and 60% bond index mutual funds for conservative, long-term investors.

Simple Portfolio Approach:

- 40% U.S. total stock index mutual fund
- 60% U.S. total bond index mutual fund

Focused Portfolio Approach:

- 20% U.S. S&P 500 stock index mutual fund
- 10% U.S. mid-capitalization stock index mutual fund
- 10% U.S. small-capitalization stock index mutual fund
- 20% U.S. long-term bond index mutual fund

- 20% U.S. intermediate-term bond index mutual fund
- 20% U.S. short-term bond index mutual fund

Targeted average annual rate of return: +7.5%.

Targeted level of volatility: Moderate level of volatility with targeted high and low annual rates of return of +25% and -20%.

- **PORTFOLIO TYPE #5** – A portfolio that consists of 20% stock index mutual funds and 80% bond index mutual funds for very conservative, long-term investors.

Simple Portfolio Approach:

- 20% U.S. total stock index mutual fund
- 80% U.S. total bond index mutual fund

Focused Portfolio Approach:

- 10% U.S. S&P 500 stock index mutual fund
- 5% U.S. mid-capitalization stock index mutual fund
- 5% U.S. small-capitalization stock index mutual fund
- 20% U.S. long-term bond index mutual fund
- 30% U.S. intermediate-term bond index mutual fund
- 30% U.S. short-term bond index mutual fund

Targeted average annual rate of return: +6.5%.

Targeted level of volatility: Moderate level of volatility with targeted high and low annual rates of return of +30% and -10%.

Choose a Mutual Fund Family

Once you have selected the portfolio of index mutual funds in which you wish to invest, it is necessary to choose a mutual fund family and the specific index mutual funds sold by the mutual fund family. Since you will be entrusting your hard-earned money to the mutual fund family, you will want to evaluate various fund families and choose one that meets your needs. You should consider the following attributes in selecting a mutual fund family.

- **Variety of Index Mutual Funds** – Does the mutual fund family have a large selection of index mutual funds, including the core index mutual funds, from which you can build a long-term investment portfolio? Some mutual fund families are known specifically for index mutual funds and offer a greater variety of such funds. Other mutual fund families may put greater emphasis on actively managed mutual funds and have fewer index mutual funds from which to choose.

- **Expenses** – As discussed in detail in previous chapters, it is extremely important to choose a mutual fund family that operates at a very low cost. Keeping expenses low means more of your investment remains in your index mutual funds. Choose a mutual fund family that offers no-load index mutual funds and has low expense ratios, generally in the range of 0.1% to 0.3%.

- **Administration and Record Keeping** – How well does the mutual fund family administer its index mutual funds and record transaction and cost basis information for tax purposes? You will want to choose a mutual fund family that does this well, provides timely reporting, and allows you to receive electronic statements securely.

- **Quality of Customer Service Support** – Is the mutual fund family known for great customer service? Inquire about the knowledge and background of their customer service support personnel. When you call for assistance, you will want to know you can rely on customer support staff that is knowledgeable about the index mutual funds offered. A great way to determine this is to call customer service and ask questions about the index mutual funds and experience first-hand the quality of the support personnel.

- **Business Hours** – Make sure the mutual fund family has business hours that meet your needs. If you are working during daytime business hours, it will be helpful to deal with a mutual fund family that provides support on the evenings and weekends.

- **Website** – How user-friendly is the mutual fund family's website? Visit the website and determine whether or not you find it easy to navigate. Ensure the website allows you to self-service your account so that you can make purchases online from your bank account, exchange shares of index mutual funds, make changes to your contact information and designate beneficiaries. Confirm the website provides for a secure mail account so that you can receive electronic transaction confirmations, quarterly statements, and year-end tax statements. Also, determine how informative the website is about the index mutual funds offered and if it provides educational articles and tools you might find helpful.

- **Quality of Prospectuses and Annual Statements** – Last but not necessarily least, you want to choose a mutual fund family that provides prospectuses and annual statements that are easy to read. Although you will likely not read these statements from cover to cover when you receive them, it will be important for you to review them from time to time. Make sure they are easy to read and provide a quick summary statement so that you can glean the important information about the index mutual fund.

Review the Index Mutual Fund Prospectus

Before you invest in a specific index mutual fund offered by the mutual fund family, you should review the index mutual fund prospectus. The prospectus provides a great deal of information. Though portions of the prospectus are tedious to read, you should read certain sections to confirm you are investing in an index mutual fund and to better understand how your money will be invested. Important sections of the prospectus include the following:

- **Investment Objective** – This section of the prospectus describes the investment goal the index mutual fund is attempting to achieve. An index mutual fund will state that the objective is to track the performance of a benchmark index such as one that measures the investment return of large-capitalization, mid-capitalization, or small-capitalization stocks. If the mutual fund were actively managed, on the other hand, the investment objective would be to provide an investment return that is greater than the performance of a benchmark index.

- **Fees and Expenses** – This section will describe the fees and expenses you will pay when you buy and hold shares of the index mutual fund, including whether or not any loads are imposed on investments or redemptions. A well-managed index mutual fund will have an expense ratio in the range of 0.1% to 0.3%. Actively managed mutual funds may have expense ratios as high as 3%.

- **Portfolio Turnover** – This section will tell you what the index mutual fund's portfolio turnover rate was in the preceding year. A fund pays transaction fees when it buys and sells shares. A higher portfolio turnover rate results in higher transaction fees, which lower a mutual fund's performance. A higher turnover rate can also result in greater capital gains distributions and taxes you will owe on those distributions. Large-capitalization stock index mutual funds will have a turnover rate in the range of 3% to 10%. Mid-capitalization and small-capitalization stock index mutual funds will have a higher turnover rate, perhaps as high as 50%. Bond index mutual funds will have a turnover rate in the range of 50% to 70%. Actively managed mutual funds will usually have much higher turnover rates, often over 100%, as the portfolio manager buys and sells stocks and bonds in an attempt to beat the market index.

- **Investment Strategy** – This section will state how the index mutual fund will achieve its investment objective and describe what investments will be made by the fund. The strategy will state the index that the index mutual fund will attempt to match. An actively managed mutual fund will have a strategy to outperform a specific index.

- **Investment Risks** – This section will describe the various financial risks that can result from investment in the index mutual fund, such as income risk, interest rate risk, currency risk, and stock market risk among others. This section should also provide a summary of prior total annual returns so that you can assess the volatility associated with the index mutual fund.

- **Investment Adviser** – This section will provide the name of the investment advisory firm responsible for managing the index mutual fund, along with the name of the portfolio manager, their educational background, and the number of years they have been the portfolio manager.

CHAPTER TEN

Dollar Cost Average

The key to growing your money with index mutual funds is to invest in them on a long-term basis, for a period of 10 or more years. When you invest long-term, it is very important to realize long-term investing is not speculating. It is not gambling. It does not involve day trading. It does not involve random moves in and out of your index mutual funds. Long-term investing involves selecting an asset allocation strategy and specific index mutual funds and sticking with your plan and investments through market highs and market lows.

When you invest for the long term, you do not want to become preoccupied with the day-to-day movements and fluctuations of the stock and bond markets. Over periods of 10, 20, and 30 years, the value of your investment in index mutual funds will have an upward trajectory. Over short-term periods, however, it may not. Over the short term, the value of investments in index mutual funds will zigzag. The value will move up. The value will move down. It is important to think of these short-term movements as noise that you should ignore. When you invest long-term, it is important to keep your eye on the future, the long term. If you do not ignore the short-term, day-to-day noise, you might very well be tempted to sell your investments against your better interests.

The most efficient means of investing in your index mutual funds is to dollar cost average into the funds. When you dollar cost average, you invest a fixed dollar amount in your index mutual funds on a consistent and ongoing basis.

For example, as a typical long-term investor utilizing a dollar cost averaging plan, you might choose to invest $500 per month in five index mutual funds, allocating $100 into each of the five funds. Each $100 invested in the index mutual fund will purchase a certain number of shares, depending on the fund price. If a fund price is $20 per share, the $100 investment will purchase [$100 / $20 per share] or 5 shares of the index mutual fund. As the fund price increases, the $100 investment will purchase a smaller number of shares of the index mutual fund. As a fund price decreases, the $100 investment will purchase a greater number of shares.

Table 10-1 illustrates how dollar cost averaging would work over four months utilizing our example of allocating $100 per month into an index mutual fund:

Month	Amount Invested	Share Price	Shares Purchased	Total Shares Owned	Investment Value
1	$100	$20	5	5	$100
2	$100	$10	10	15	$150
3	$100	$5	20	35	$175
4	$100	$25	4	39	$975

Table 10-1 Dollar Cost Averaging Example

As you can see from the example, when the share price is $20 per share, 5 shares of the index mutual fund are purchased. When the share price rises to $25 per share, only 4 shares of the index mutual fund are purchased. Also note, that when the share price is $25 per share, the 20 shares that were purchased when the share price was only $5 per share, increase dramatically in value to $500. That is the beauty of dollar cost averaging. It enables you to buy a greater number of shares when the share price is low. It also forces you to buy fewer shares when the share price is high. As an investor, this is what you want to do. Dollar cost averaging is an excellent way to invest. It compels you to continually invest through good times and bad. Because you are continually investing, dollar cost averaging also removes the fear many investors have of investing at the wrong time.

As mentioned previously, there will be times when the markets zigzag and drop precipitously in value. Do not be tempted to outsmart the markets, however, by withdrawing money from your index mutual funds during a stock or bond market decline—no matter how bad or painful it may feel. Many investors think they can outsmart the market. They will pull their investments from their index mutual funds during a stock or bond market decline intending to reinvest the money at the stock or bond market bottom. Those who do pull their money out of their index mutual funds often miss a future advance in stock or bond market prices. By the time they reinvest, a fast-moving stock or bond market has realized much of its gains. Such foolish investors often end up selling low and buying high, and that is not a good investment strategy.

Accept the fact you are investing for the long term. Continue to invest during market fluctuations. If you choose a mutual fund family with low expenses and stick to your asset allocation and index mutual fund selections through good times and bad, you should do very well with your investments over time.

When you dollar cost average, you should select an investment cycle that works for you. You can choose to invest weekly, bi-weekly, monthly, or quarterly. Most mutual fund families will allow you to set up an automatic withdrawal from your bank checking or savings account to be deposited into your index mutual fund. There is no one investment cycle better than another. Whether you invest each time you are paid at work, the first day of the month, or the last day of the quarter, it generally will not make a difference over the long haul. The important point is to invest on a regular, uninterrupted basis, through market highs and market lows. Invest, invest, invest, and after many years, you will find you have grown your money and captured wealth.

CHAPTER ELEVEN

Establish a Cost Basis Methodology

At the time you begin to invest in your index mutual fund, you should select a cost basis methodology for the index mutual funds. The cost basis is effectively what you have paid for your shares of the fund. For example, if you make an initial investment of $5,000 in your index mutual fund, your initial cost basis will be $5,000. If you make additional investments, your cost basis will increase by the amount of those additional investments. If you receive dividend distributions or capital gains distributions from your index mutual fund and have those payments reinvested in it, your cost basis will increase by the amount of the reinvested distributions. An increase in the value of your index mutual fund shares due to capital appreciation does not increase your cost basis.

Table 11-1 shows an example of payments into an index mutual fund and the corresponding cost basis:

Investment	Cost Basis
$ 5,000 Contribution	$5,000
$ 300 Dividend Distribution Reinvestment	$5,300
$ 200 Capital Gains Distribution Reinvestment	$5,500

Table 11-1 Index Mutual Fund Cost Basis Example

The reason you need to establish a cost basis methodology is that you need to report to the Internal Revenue Service (IRS) capital gains and losses incurred when you sell shares of your index mutual funds. For example, in the preceding scenario, the investor has invested $5,000 and reinvested $300 in dividend distributions and $200 in capital gains distributions for a total investment or cost basis of $5,500. If the investor were to sell the shares in the index mutual fund for $7,500, they would have to report a capital gain to the IRS of [$7,500 - $5,500] or $2,000, which is determined by subtracting the cost basis from the proceeds of the sale. Short-term capital gains tax rates apply to the sale of shares in an index mutual fund held for one year or less. Long-term capital gains tax rates apply to the sale of shares in an index mutual fund held longer than one year. If an investor were to sell shares for less than the cost basis, they would be able to claim a capital loss. The cost basis methodology will determine what the cost basis is for capital gain and capital loss tax reporting purposes.

There are three primary options from which to choose when selecting a cost basis methodology. Each varies in terms of flexibility in reporting gains and losses and record-keeping complexity. Following is a description of each cost basis methodology:

- **Average Cost Methodology** – The average cost methodology utilizes an average cost per share owned. To determine your cost basis under this methodology, you simply add up the total amount you paid for all shares and divide by the total number of shares owned. Under this methodology, each share has the same cost basis per share and provides the simplest means of determining the per-share cost basis. This methodology will likely require little record keeping on your part as most mutual fund families will provide complete cost basis information for this methodology to the IRS. The downside to this methodology is that it does not provide flexibility in taxable gain and loss reporting. Because each share has the same average cost basis, you will not be able to minimize taxable gains or maximize taxable losses by selling those shares purchased at your highest cost.

- **First-In, First-Out Methodology** – The first-in, first-out methodology applies a specific cost basis for each share. Under this methodology, the cost basis for each share is equal to what you paid for it. The first-in, first-out methodology assumes, however, that the first shares purchased are the first shares sold. Other than the fact it might be easy to conceptualize and understand, this methodology has few advantages compared to the other two methodologies. It requires detailed record keeping of the purchase price for each share owned. Some mutual fund families will not provide this information to the IRS, and it will be up to you to do so. Like the average cost methodology, it provides no flexibility in taxable gain and loss reporting. Because you cannot select the specific shares you are selling at a given time, the first shares purchased must be the first shares sold, you will not be able to minimize taxable gains or maximize taxable losses by selling those shares with the highest cost basis.

- **Specific Identification Methodology** – The specific identification methodology applies a specific cost basis for each share. Under this methodology, the cost basis for each share is equal to what you paid for it. With this methodology, you can also specify exactly which shares you want to sell at any given time. The downside to this methodology is it requires detailed record keeping of the purchase price for each share owned. Some mutual fund families will not provide this information to the IRS, and it will be up to you to do so. The advantage of this methodology is it provides the greatest flexibility in taxable gain and loss reporting. Because it allows you to select the specific shares of your index mutual fund that you want to sell, you will be able to minimize taxable gains and maximize taxable losses. For example, if you want to minimize the tax due on capital gains or maximize capital losses, you can sell the shares of the index mutual fund with the highest cost basis.

Examples of Cost Basis Methodologies

Following are examples of each cost basis methodology to help you better visualize how each works. By reviewing the examples, you will have a better understanding of the impact each methodology has on the cost basis of each share of an index mutual fund and the corresponding taxable gain. The examples for each methodology utilize the same purchase dates, investment amounts, cost per share, and the number of shares purchased. You will see, however, that each methodology results in a different taxable gain. More specifically, you will see the specific identification methodology that provides the greatest flexibility in choosing the shares sold and enables you to increase your cost basis and reduce your tax liability in certain circumstances.

Taking advantage of this flexibility, however, requires greater administrative work and per-share price tracking of each share purchased.

Average Cost Methodology Example

In this example, 135 shares of an index mutual fund are purchased on three separate dates at various per-share prices as shown in Table 11-2.

Purchase Date	Investment	Cost Per Share	# of Shares Purchased
1/1/2022	$5,000	$40	125
6/1/2022	$300	$50	6
9/1/2022	$208	$52	4

Table 11-2 Purchase Schedule for Cost Basis Methodology Examples

With the average cost methodology, the cost basis per share is the same for each of the shares owned no matter when the shares were purchased or for what price. In this example, the total cost basis is $5,508, or $40.80 per share [$5,508/135 shares]. If 50 of the 135 shares are sold, the cost basis of the 50 shares sold would be [50 shares x $40.80] or $2,040. If the 50 shares were sold at $60 per share for $3,000, the taxable gain would be $960, the difference between the sale price of the 50 shares ($3,000) and their cost basis ($2,040).

First-In, First-Out Methodology Example

As in the prior example, 135 shares of an index mutual fund are purchased on three separate dates at various per-share prices as shown in Table 11-2.

With the first-in, first-out methodology, the cost basis per share is determined separately at the time the shares are purchased. The shares purchased on 1/1/2022 have a cost basis per share of [$5,000 / 125 shares] or $40. The shares purchased on 6/1/2022 have a cost basis per share of [$300 / 6 shares] or $50. The shares purchased on 9/1/2022 have a cost basis per share of [$208/4 shares] or $52. If 50 of the 135 shares are sold, the shares sold would be 50 of the 125 shares purchased on 1/1/2022. These represent the first shares purchased and, thus, will be the first shares sold. The cost basis of the 50 shares sold would be [50 shares x $40 per share] or $2,000. If the 50 shares were sold at $60 per share for $3,000, the taxable gain would be $1,000, the difference between the sale price of the 50 shares ($3,000) and their cost basis ($2,000). As you can see, in this particular example, the first-in, first-out methodology results in a taxable gain that is greater than the taxable gain generated using the average cost methodology.

Specific Identification Methodology Example

As in the prior examples, 135 shares of an index mutual fund are purchased on three separate dates at various per-share prices as shown in Table 11-2.

With the specific identification methodology, the cost basis per share is determined separately at the time the shares are purchased, just as in the first-in, first-out methodology. The shares purchased on 1/1/2022 have a cost basis per share of [$5,000 / 125 shares] or $40. The shares purchased on 6/1/2022 have a cost basis per share of [$300 / 6 shares] or $50. The shares purchased on 9/1/2022 have a cost basis per share of [$208 / 4 shares] or $52. With the specific identification methodology, however, you have greater flexibility in selecting the specific shares that are sold, which can allow you to increase the cost basis and reduce the taxable gain.

Thus, if 50 of the 135 shares are sold, the 50 shares can consist of the 4 shares purchased on 9/1/2022 with a cost basis of $52 per share, 6 shares purchased on 6/1/2022 with a cost basis of $50 per share, and 40 shares purchased on 1/1/2022 with a cost basis of $40 per share. The cost basis of the 50 shares sold would be [(4 shares x $52) + (6 shares x $50) + (40 shares x $40)] or $2,108. If the 50 shares were sold at $60 per share for $3,000, the taxable gain would be $892, the difference between the sale price of the 50 shares ($3,000) and their cost basis ($2,108). As you can see, in this particular example, the specific identification methodology results in a taxable gain that is less than the taxable gain generated using the other two methodologies.

Choosing a Cost Basis Methodology

Choosing a cost basis methodology is a personal choice between you and your tax preparer. For most investors, the average cost methodology is likely the best option as it is easy to understand, requires the least amount of record keeping, and treats all shares equally for tax purposes at the time of sale. If having greater control over your taxable gains and taxable losses is important to you, then the specific identification methodology may be the best methodology for you. Just keep in mind that taking advantage of this flexibility requires greater administrative work and tracking of the per-share price of each share purchased.

CHAPTER TWELVE

Rebalance

It is important to evaluate your long-term investment portfolio on an ongoing basis to ensure it continues to be in line with your desired asset allocation. Your asset allocation is chosen based on your level of risk tolerance and other factors, such as the stability of your income and the existence of an emergency fund. Assuming these factors remain unchanged, your asset allocation should remain unchanged as well, and therefore, it is important to verify that your long-term investments continue to meet your targeted asset allocation.

For example, assume you selected a moderate asset allocation of 60% stock index mutual funds and 40% bond index mutual funds. However, due to an increase in the value of your stock index mutual funds, your asset allocation shifted to an aggressive asset allocation of 80% stock index mutual funds and 20% bond index mutual funds. As we saw in Chapter Six, an investment portfolio of 80% stock index mutual funds and 20% bond index mutual funds is going to be more volatile than a portfolio of 60% stock index mutual funds and 40% bond index mutual funds. A portfolio of 80% stock index mutual funds and 20% bond index mutual funds has a targeted, average, annual rate of return of 9.0% with a targeted high and low annual rate of return of +45% and -35%. A portfolio of 60%

stock index mutual funds and 40% bond index mutual funds has a targeted, average, annual rate of return of 8.5% with a targeted high and low annual rate of return of +35% and -30%.

If your risk profile remains unchanged, then a portfolio of 80% stock index mutual funds and 20% bond index mutual funds will be too volatile for you. So you do not experience volatility with which you are not comfortable, you would need to adjust your holdings in your index mutual funds, such that your asset allocation is once again 60% stock index mutual funds and 40% bond index mutual funds.

In this example, to bring your asset allocation back in line with your risk profile, you would sell portions of your stock index mutual funds and purchase additional shares of your bond index mutual funds. Doing so will bring your asset allocation back to your targeted asset allocation and to your volatility comfort level.

For example, assuming your asset allocation has adjusted to 80% stock index mutual funds and 20% bond index mutual funds, your investment portfolio might be as shown in Table 12-1.

Asset Allocation	Investment Portfolio	Investment Amount
80% Stock Index Mutual Funds	50% U.S. Total Stock Index Mutual Fund	$50,000
	30% Foreign Total Stock Index Mutual Fund	$30,000
20% Bond Index Mutual Funds	15% U.S. Total Bond Index Mutual Fund	$15,000
	5% Foreign Total Bond Index Mutual Fund	$5,000

Table 12-1 Moderate Asset Allocation Portfolio Before Rebalancing

Assuming a desired asset allocation of 60% stock index mutual funds and 40% bond index mutual funds, however, you would want to sell shares in the two stock index mutual funds and buy additional shares in the two bond index mutual funds. The specific amounts bought and sold should reestablish the percentage mix of the index mutual funds for the portfolio you selected. Assuming the chosen portfolio in this example is Portfolio Type #3 – Simple Portfolio Approach, the value in each index mutual fund would be rebalanced as shown in Table 12-2.

Asset Allocation	Investment Portfolio	Investment Amount
60% Stock Index Mutual Funds	40% U.S. Total Stock Index Mutual Fund	$40,000
	20% Foreign Total Stock Index Mutual Fund	$20,000
40% Bond Index Mutual Funds	30% U.S. Total Bond Index Mutual Fund	$30,000
	10% Foreign Total Bond Index Mutual Fund	$10,000

Table 12-2 Moderate Asset Allocation Portfolio After Rebalancing

By selling shares in the stock index mutual funds and purchasing shares in the bond index mutual funds, you have decreased the amount of your investment in stock funds from $80,000 to $60,000 and increased the amount of your investment in the bond funds to $40,000 from $20,000. Doing so readjusts the asset allocation from 80% stock funds and 20% bond funds to 60% stock funds and 40% bond funds. This reestablishes the desired asset allocation and investment portfolio to a level of volatility that is acceptable and in line with your risk profile.

In addition to ensuring you are not taking on investment risk with which you are not comfortable, rebalancing your assets drives you to sell high and buy low. In the example shown, the stock portion of the investment portfolio grew to 80% of the portfolio because the stock index mutual funds increased in value. By rebalancing the portfolio and selling shares of the stock index mutual funds, you are selling shares when they are highly valued and buying shares of the bond index mutual funds when they are less expensive. When investing long-term, you want to buy low and sell high. Rebalancing helps you to do this.

How Often Should You Rebalance?

Rebalancing should be done annually, though it can be done on a semi-annual basis if desired. Variations of a few percentage points to your asset allocation can be overlooked, but variations of 5% or more should be addressed.

CHAPTER THIRTEEN

Tax-Advantaged Personal Investment Plans

When investing for the long term, it is important to take advantage of tax-advantaged personal investment plans, such as the Roth 401(k), the traditional 401(k), the Roth IRA, and the traditional IRA. Utilizing these plans will allow you to grow your money to a greater level of wealth and should be utilized as part of your overall investment portfolio.

A **Roth 401(k)** plan enables you to invest after-tax income in an investment plan offered by your employer. There are no income restrictions to participate. Qualified withdrawals of contributions and the earnings on those contributions may be withdrawn tax-free as long as you have participated in the plan for at least five years and you are at least fifty-nine and a half years old. Non-qualified withdrawals taken before you have participated in the plan for five years or before turning fifty-nine and a half years old are subject to a 10 percent penalty and taxation on the earnings portion of the withdrawal. There are no taxes or penalties on the contribution portion of a withdrawal. Contribution limits apply. An RMD, which stands for Required Minimum Distribution and is the minimum amount that must be withdrawn from certain retirement accounts each year, is not required.

A **traditional 401(k)** plan enables you to invest pre-tax income in an investment plan offered by your employer. There are no income restrictions to participate. Qualified withdrawals of contributions and earnings may be taken at age fifty-nine and a half and later and are taxed at ordinary income tax rates in effect at the time of the withdrawal without penalty. A non-qualified withdrawal taken before the age of fifty-nine and a half will be subject to a 10 percent penalty in addition to being taxed as ordinary income. Contribution limits apply. RMDs must commence by age seventy-three if you were born between 1951 and 1959, and by age seventy-five if you were born in 1960 or later.

A big plus for many 401(k) plans, both Roth and traditional, is the company match. Many employers will match your contributions to the plans up to a certain percentage of your salary. For example, if your employer offers a 3 percent company match, it will contribute a dollar to your 401(k) plan for each dollar you contribute up to 3 percent of your salary. A company match is a great benefit and if your employer offers one, you should contribute to your Roth 401(k) or traditional 401(k) at a minimum of the company match to take full advantage of the benefit. It should be noted that nonprofit organizations offer 403(b) plans rather than 401(k) plans. These plans work much the same way as 401(k) plans offered by for-profit companies.

In addition to employer-sponsored 401(k) and 403(b) plans, the tax code provides for tax-advantaged investing using a Roth IRA and traditional IRA.

A **Roth IRA** enables you to invest after-tax income in an investment plan of your choosing. Qualified withdrawals of your contributions and the earnings on those contributions may be withdrawn tax-free as long as you have participated in the plan for at least five years and you are at least fifty-nine and a half years old. Non-qualified withdrawals taken before you have participated in the plan for five years or before turning fifty-nine and a half years old are subject to a 10 percent penalty and taxation at ordinary income tax rates on the earnings portion of the withdrawal. There are no taxes or penalties on the contribution portion of a withdrawal. Income limits and contribution limits apply. An RMD is not required.

A **traditional IRA** enables you to contribute to an investment plan of your choosing. Contributions may or may not be tax deductible depending on your income level and whether or not you are active in an employer retirement plan. If you are not active in an employer retirement plan, contributions are fully deductible regardless of your income. If you are active in an employer retirement plan, your contributions are deductible only if your income is less than certain income limits. Qualified withdrawals of deductible contributions and earnings are taxed at ordinary income tax rates in effect at the time of the withdrawal. A non-qualified withdrawal taken before the age of fifty-nine and a half will also be subject to a 10 percent penalty. Withdrawal of any nondeductible contributions are considered basis and are not taxed or penalized as long as they have been reported as such to the IRS on IRS Form 8606 for the year the contribution was made. Contribution limits apply. RMDs must commence by age seventy-three if you were born between 1951 and 1959 and by age seventy-five if you were born in 1960 or later.

CHAPTER FOURTEEN

Seek Assistance from a Fee-Only Financial Planner

Growing your money through index mutual funds may seem overwhelming at times. If you need assistance, engage a fee-only financial planner to help you. A fee-only financial planner will charge a flat fee or hourly rate for his or her services. They will offer unbiased, professional, client-focused advice and will be able to assist you in selecting a portfolio of low-cost index mutual funds that will help you attain your long-term investment goals.

When choosing a fee-only financial planner to assist you, look for one who holds a degree in personal financial planning from an accredited college or university. Many colleges and universities offer programs in personal financial planning and confer bachelor of science degrees, master of science degrees, and doctor of philosophy degrees in personal financial planning.

The fee-only financial planner you choose should also hold the chartered financial consultant designation (ChFC) and/or the certified financial planner designation (CFP). Chartered financial consultant and certified financial planner designee holders have completed rigorous coursework and a series of examinations in personal financial planning. They are also required to complete continuing education requirements and meet ethical code of conduct standards.

Equally important to finding a fee-only financial planner knowledgeable in the practice of financial planning is finding a planner with whom you are comfortable. It is very important you be able to communicate with your planner. You must trust that they listen to you and understand your needs. Likewise, your planner must be able to communicate in a manner that is understandable to you. The fee-only financial planner you choose should be able to explain the index mutual funds in which they will have you invest and why the funds belong in your long-term investment portfolio. They should agree to meet with you on a quarterly or semi-annual basis to discuss the status of your long-term investment portfolio.

Remember, the planner you hire is going to work for you and manage an extremely important aspect of your life. Take your time when selecting one, interview multiple candidates, and be comfortable with your choice.

PART THREE

Case Studies

CHAPTER FIFTEEN

Case Study: Rachel, a 28-Year-Old Physical Therapist

Rachel is a 28-year-old physical therapist who earns $90,000 annually. She owns a townhome near the hospital at which she works. She purchased the townhome with a 20% down payment which has allowed her to keep her monthly housing expenses low, relative to her income. She also enjoys a simple life. She cycles on the weekends with friends and volunteers at a nearby animal shelter. She also prefers to cook a healthy meal at home rather than spend money on costly meals at restaurants. Rachel already invests the maximum amount in her hospital's retirement plan. Because she lives modestly and well within her means, she finds she has discretionary income that she would like to invest toward her retirement. She would like to grow her money and invest $300 per week in index mutual funds.

Rachel considers herself to be a moderate risk-taker, but she does not think she would be too happy if she saw a large drop in the value of her retirement fund. She has a six-month emergency fund in place and a small car loan outstanding in addition to the mortgage on her townhome. Other than investments in the hospital's retirement plan, she does not believe she has much experience with investments and thinks her knowledge of investments is very limited.

To help her better assess her personal risk profile, Rachel first completes the Risk Assessment Questionnaire as follows:

Rachel's Risk Assessment Questionnaire Results

Question #1: What is your age?
- A. **35 years and younger**
- B. 36 to 54 years
- C. 55 to 64 years
- D. 65 years and older

Question #2: When do you expect to use the money you are now planning to invest?
- A. **In more than 20 years**
- B. In 11 to 20 years
- C. In 5 to 10 years
- D. In less than 5 years

Question #3: Over what length of time do you expect to spend the money once you begin to withdraw from the investment portfolio?
- A. **More than 20 years**
- B. 11 to 20 years
- C. 5 to 10 years
- D. Less than 5 years

Question #4: How would you describe your future income over the next several years?
   A. **Very reliable**
   B. Reliable
   C. Unreliable
   D. Very unreliable

Question #5: Do you have an emergency fund in place and for how long will it cover your expenses in the event of a job loss?
   A. Yes, more than 2 years
   B. **Yes, 6 months to 2 years**
   C. Yes, less than 6 months
   D. No, I do not have an emergency fund

Question #6: How would you describe your level of debt?
   A. I do not have debt
   B. I have a small amount of debt
   C. **I have a fair amount of debt**
   D. I have a significant amount of debt

Question #7: How would you describe your understanding of investments?
   A. Excellent
   B. Good
   C. Limited
   D. **Extremely limited**

Question #8: How many years of experience do you have with investment products?

    A. More than 20 years
    B. 11 to 20 years
    C. 5 to 10 years
    D. **Less than 5 years**

Question #9: In the past, when you have experienced a surprising change in your life that presented challenges, such as losing a job or being forced to relocate, were you:

    A. Excited about a new opportunity
    B. **Concerned about the change, but able to manage the situation**
    C. Initially unhappy but eventually able to cope
    D. Extremely unhappy and emotionally stressed

Question #10: If you are a contestant on a game show and have the choice of keeping $10,000 or winning more, which do you choose?

    A. A 10% chance of winning $100,000
    B. A 25% chance of winning $50,000
    C. **A 50% chance of winning $20,000**
    D. The $10,000

Question #11: Which investment portfolio would you choose?

    A. Portfolio A: Earns either a 50% return or a 25% loss
    B. Portfolio B: Earns either a 30% return or a 15% loss
    C. **Portfolio C: Earns either a 15% return or a 7% loss**
    D. Portfolio D: Earns either an 8% return or a 3% loss

Question #12: If your investment portfolio lost 30% of its value in two months, how long would you wait for your investment portfolio to regain its value?

A. 2 years or more
B. **More than 1 year but less than 2 years**
C. 6 months to a 1 year
D. Less than 6 months

Question #13: Which investment portfolio would you prefer?

A. Portfolio A: 10% return with a high degree of volatility to principal
B. **Portfolio B: 7% return with a medium degree of volatility to principal**
C. Portfolio C: 5% return with a low degree of volatility to principal
D. Portfolio D: 3% return with no volatility to principal

Question #14: If there was a severe economic crisis and the value of your investment portfolio decreased by 50%, what would you do?

A. Leave the investment portfolio as is and continue making additional investments as planned
B. Leave the investment portfolio as is but stop making additional investments
C. **Move a portion of the investment portfolio from more risky stock index mutual funds to less risky bond index mutual funds**
D. Move the investment portfolio into a federally insured, bank savings account

Question #15: What is the maximum loss in your investment portfolio that you would be comfortable with over a 6-month period?

    A. 40% to 50% decline
    B. 25% to 30% decline
    C. 10% to 15% decline
    D. 0% to 5% decline

After completing the questionnaire, Rachel determines her score by giving herself four points for the questions she answered with A, three points for questions she answered with B, two points for questions she answered with C, and one point for questions she answered with D. She determines her score is 41 points, which classifies Rachel as a moderate risk-taker. Rachel believes the results of the questionnaire are reasonable and in line with how she views her level of risk tolerance.

After completing the Risk Assessment Questionnaire, the next step is to select an asset allocation for her investment portfolio. Before doing so, Rachel evaluates the various asset allocation models. She looks at the average annual rates of return and, more importantly, the volatility associated with each model. She decides to select the Moderate Asset Allocation, Model C, which is the asset allocation suggested by the Risk Assessment Questionnaire and the one with which she is most comfortable.

MODEL C – Moderate Asset Allocation:

- % Stock Index Mutual Fund: 60%
- % Bond Index Mutual Fund: 40%

- Targeted Average Annual Rate of Return: +8.5%
- Targeted High Annual Rate of Return: + 35%
- Targeted Low Annual Rate of Return: - 30%

Now that Rachel has decided upon an asset allocation model, she is ready to choose a portfolio of index mutual funds. As a moderate investor with the desired asset allocation of 60% stock index mutual funds and 40% bond index mutual funds, Rachel chooses Portfolio Type #3, a portfolio for moderate, long-term investors. Rachel sees she has a choice between the Simple Portfolio Approach and the Focused Portfolio Approach. Rachel prefers to keep her finances as simple as possible and to keep the administration of her index mutual funds to a minimum. She chooses the Simple Portfolio Approach and decides to invest in the following index mutual funds:

PORTFOLIO TYPE #3 – Simple Portfolio Approach for Moderate Investors:

- 40% in the U.S. total stock index mutual fund
- 20% in the foreign total stock index mutual fund
- 30% in the U.S. total bond index mutual fund
- 10% in the foreign total bond index mutual fund

Now that she has decided on which index mutual funds she will invest in, Rachel needs to select a mutual fund family. After reviewing a few, she chooses one that has been in business for many years. The mutual fund family has a solid reputation for no-load, index mutual funds and for keeping fund expenses to a minimum. The average expense ratio for their index mutual funds is a low 0.2%. She also finds the website for the mutual fund family to be user-friendly. It provides an in-depth analysis of each index mutual fund and also includes tutorials on investing long-term with mutual funds.

Rachel is comfortable investing $300 per week in her index mutual funds after making the required minimum initial investment of $2,000 in each of her four index mutual funds. She sets up an automatic investment plan with the mutual fund family and her bank. She decides to dollar cost average in the four index mutual funds as follows:

- $120 (40% of $300) per week in the U.S. total stock index mutual fund

- $60 (20% of $300) per week in the foreign total stock index mutual fund

- $90 (30% of $300) per week in the U.S. total bond index mutual fund

- $30 (10% of $300) per week in the foreign total bond index mutual fund

With her index mutual funds selected and having reviewed the prospectus for each, Rachel just needs to select a cost basis methodology. Again, being one to keep things simple, Rachel chooses the average cost methodology for each index mutual fund. With the average cost methodology, each share within each fund will have the same cost basis, and Rachel will be able to rely on her mutual fund family to provide the necessary cost basis information for tax purposes.

Rachel is very satisfied with her index mutual fund selections and her long-term investment plan. She anticipates investing for 32 years. The expected annual average rate of return for her moderate investor asset allocation and investment portfolio is 8.5%.

If Rachel initially invests the minimum requirement of $2,000 in each of her four index mutual funds, for a total initial investment of $8,000, and continues to contribute $300 per week in her portfolio over 32 years, and she earns an average annualized rate of return of 8.3% on her investments (8.5% earned by her investment portfolio less 0.2% for expenses charged by the mutual fund), she will grow her money to $2,596,046 at the end of 32 years.

Note: The accumulated value assumes income taxes due on dividends and capital gain distributions are paid annually out of pocket, outside of the investment portfolio.

CHAPTER SIXTEEN

Case Study: Alex, a 25-Year-Old Computer Programmer

Alex is a 25-year-old computer programmer who earns $110,000 per year working for a commodities brokerage company. He owns a condominium and has a low mortgage payment relative to his income. He has more than two years' worth of living expenses in an emergency fund. Alex enjoys a simple life and is, thus, able to keep expenses to a minimum. He spends his free time swimming and exercising at the local YMCA and enjoys backpacking and camping for vacation. Alex minored in economics in college and enjoys reading books and articles on investments. He already invests the maximum allowed in tax-advantaged personal investment plans and is looking to grow his money further so that he can retire comfortably at age 65. He has savings set aside in addition to his emergency fund to make an initial investment and believes he can afford to invest $400 per week in a personal investment portfolio on an ongoing basis.

Alex considers himself to be an aggressive risk-taker with regard to long-term investments. He realizes he has time on his side and that over the long term, his investments will grow substantially. He studies the stock and bond markets and realizes there are up and down cycles. He is not concerned about short-term fluctuations and thinks he can withstand intermittent drops in the value of his investment portfolio, even losses of value that are substantial. To better assess his risk profile, Alex completes the Risk Assessment Questionnaire as follows:

Alex's Risk Assessment Questionnaire Results

Question #1: What is your age?
- A. **35 years or younger**
- B. 36 to 54 years
- C. 55 to 64 years
- D. 65 years or older

Question #2: When do you expect to use the money you are now planning to invest?
- A. **In more than 20 years**
- B. In 11 to 20 years
- C. In 5 to 10 years
- D. In less than 5 years

Question #3: Over what length of time do you expect to spend the money once you begin to withdraw from the investment portfolio?
- A. **More than 20 years**
- B. 11 to 20 years
- C. 5 to 10 years
- D. Less than 5 years

Question #4: How would you describe your future income over the next several years?

    A. **Very reliable**
    B. Reliable
    C. Unreliable
    D. Very unreliable

Question #5: Do you have an emergency fund in place and for how long will it cover your expenses in the event of a job loss?

    A. **Yes, more than 2 years**
    B. Yes, 6 months to 2 years
    C. Yes, less than 6 months
    D. No, I do not have an emergency fund

Question #6: How would you describe your level of debt?

    A. I do not have debt
    B. **I have a small amount of debt**
    C. I have a fair amount of debt
    D. I have a significant amount of debt

Question #7: How would you describe your understanding of investments?

    A. **Excellent**
    B. Good
    C. Limited
    D. Extremely limited

Question #8: How many years of experience do you have with investment products?

    A. More than 20 years
    B. 11 to 20 years
    C. **5 to 10 years**
    D. Less than 5 years

Question #9: In the past, when you have experienced a surprising change in your life that presented challenges, such as losing a job or being forced to relocate, were you:

    A. **Excited about a new opportunity**
    B. Concerned about the change, but able to manage the situation
    C. Initially unhappy but eventually able to cope
    D. Extremely unhappy and emotionally stressed

Question #10: If you are a contestant on a game show and have the choice of keeping $10,000 or winning more, which do you choose?

    A. A 10% chance of winning $100,000
    B. **A 25% chance of winning $50,000**
    C. A 50% chance of winning $20,000
    D. The $10,000

Question #11: Which investment portfolio would you choose?

    A. **Portfolio A: Earns either a 50% return or a 25% loss**
    B. Portfolio B: Earns either a 30% return or a 15% loss
    C. Portfolio C: Earns either a 15% return or a 7% loss
    D. Portfolio D: Earns either an 8% return or a 3% loss

Question #12: If your investment portfolio lost 30% of its value in two months, how long would you wait for your investment portfolio to regain its value?

   A. **2 years or more**
   B. More than 1 year but less than 2 years
   C. 6 months to a 1 year
   D. Less than 6 months

Question #13: Which investment portfolio would you prefer?

   A. **Portfolio A: 10% return with a high degree of volatility to principal**
   B. Portfolio B: 7% return with a medium degree of volatility to principal
   C. Portfolio C: 5% return with a low degree of volatility to principal
   D. Portfolio D: 3% return with no volatility to principal

Question #14: If there was a severe economic crisis and the value of your investment portfolio decreased by 50%, what would you do?

   A. **Leave the investment portfolio as is and continue making additional investments as planned**
   B. Leave the investment portfolio as is but stop making additional investments
   C. Move a portion of the investment portfolio from more risky stock index mutual funds to less risky bond index mutual funds
   D. Move the investment portfolio into a federally insured, bank savings account

Question #15: What is the maximum loss in your investment portfolio that you would be comfortable with over a 6-month period?

A. **40% to 50% decline**
B. 25% to 30% decline
C. 10% to 15% decline
D. 0% to 5% decline

After completing the questionnaire, Alex determines his score by giving himself four points for the questions he answered with A, three points for questions he answered with B, two points for questions he answered with C, and one point for questions he answered with D. He determines his score is 56 points, which classifies Alex as an extremely strong risk-taker. Alex believes the results of the questionnaire are reasonable and in line with how he views himself and his willingness to take risks with his long-term investment portfolio.

After completing the Risk Assessment Questionnaire, the next step is to select an asset allocation for his investment portfolio. Before doing so, Alex evaluates the various asset allocation models. He looks at the average annual rates of return and, more importantly, the volatility associated with each model. He decides to select the Very Aggressive Asset Allocation, Model A, which is the asset allocation suggested by the Risk Assessment Questionnaire and the one with which he is most comfortable.

MODEL A – Very Aggressive Asset Allocation Model:

- % Stock Index Mutual Fund: 100%
- Targeted Average Annual Rate of Return: +9.5%

- Targeted High Annual Rate of Return: +50%
- Targeted Low Annual Rate of Return: -45%

Now that Alex has decided upon an asset allocation model, he is ready to choose a portfolio of index mutual funds. As a very aggressive investor with a desired asset allocation of 100% stocks, Alex chooses Portfolio Type #1, a portfolio for very aggressive, long-term investors. Alex sees he has a choice between the Simple Portfolio Approach and the Focused Portfolio Approach. Alex likes the idea of fine-tuning his investment choices across different segments of the stock market and chooses the Focused Portfolio Approach. Alex decides to invest in the following index mutual funds:

PORTFOLIO TYPE #1 – Focused Portfolio Approach for Very Aggressive Investors:

- 30% in the U.S. S&P 500 stock index mutual fund
- 25% in the U.S. mid-capitalization stock index mutual fund
- 25% in the U.S. small-capitalization stock index mutual fund
- 10% in the foreign developed market stock index mutual fund
- 10% in the foreign emerging market stock index mutual fund

Now that he has decided which index mutual funds he will invest in, Alex needs to select a mutual fund family.

After reviewing a few, he chooses a mutual fund family that has been in business for many years. The mutual fund family has a solid reputation for no-load, index mutual funds and for keeping fund expenses to a minimum. The average expense ratio for their index mutual funds is a low 0.2%. He also finds the website for the mutual fund family to be user-friendly. It provides an in-depth analysis of each index mutual fund and also includes tutorials on investing long-term with mutual funds.

Alex is comfortable investing $400 per week into his index mutual funds. He sets up an automatic investment plan with the mutual fund family and his bank. He decides to dollar cost average in the five index mutual funds as follows:

- $120 (30% of $400) per week in the U.S. S&P 500 stock index mutual fund

- $100 (25% of $400) per week in the U.S. mid-capitalization stock index mutual fund

- $100 (25% of $400) per week in the U.S. small-capitalization stock index mutual fund

- $40 (10% of $400) per week in the foreign developed market stock index mutual fund

- $40 (10% of $400) per week in the foreign emerging market stock index mutual fund

With his index mutual funds selected and having reviewed the prospectus for each, Alex just needs to select a cost basis methodology. After evaluating the cost basis choices, Alex chooses the average cost methodology for each fund. With the average cost methodology, each share within each fund will have the same cost basis and the mutual fund family he selected will provide all necessary record keeping.

Alex is very satisfied with his index mutual fund selections and his long-term investment plan. He anticipates investing for 40 years. The targeted, annual, average, rate of return for his very aggressive investor asset allocation and investment portfolio is 9.5%.

If Alex initially invests the minimum requirement of $3,000 in each of his five index mutual funds, for a total initial investment of $15,000, and continues to contribute $400 per week in his portfolio over 40 years, and he earns an average annualized rate of return of 9.3% on his investments (9.5% earned by his investment portfolio less 0.2% for expenses charged by the mutual fund), he will grow his money to $9,591,269 at the end of 40 years.

Note: The accumulated value assumes income taxes due on dividends and capital gain distributions are paid annually out of pocket, outside of the investment portfolio.

CHAPTER SEVENTEEN

Case Study: Tyler, a 35-Year-Old Engineer, and Claire, a 34-Year-Old English Teacher

---

Tyler is a 35-year-old engineer, and his wife Claire is a 34-year-old high school English teacher. They have twin 10-year-old boys and their combined income is $180,000 per year. They own a single-family home and have a low mortgage payment relative to their income. They have one year's worth of savings in an emergency fund. Tyler, Claire, and their boys enjoy a simple life. They prefer to cook healthy, affordable meals at home rather than go out to expensive restaurants. For vacations, they go camping and hiking, and for entertainment, they enjoy board games and reading.

Tyler occasionally reads about long-term investing but believes he has a basic and somewhat limited grasp of investing in stock and bond mutual funds. Claire's knowledge of investments is limited, as well. Tyler and Claire invest the maximum allowed in tax-advantaged personal investment plans available to them in their workplaces and recently set aside an inheritance in an insured savings account for the twins' college education. Now they would like to invest discretionary income in a personal long-term investment portfolio utilizing index mutual funds to better prepare themselves for retirement. They have enough savings set aside to make an initial investment of $6,000 and feel they can invest $350 per week on an ongoing basis in their personal investment portfolio.

Tyler and Claire consider themselves to be conservative risk-takers with regard to long-term investments. They realize time is on their side, as they do not plan to retire for another 30 years, and, over the long term, their investments will grow substantially. They recall the financial crisis of 2008, however, and fully understand stock and bond markets come with great financial risks. They know they would not be comfortable with dramatic drops in the value of their investment portfolio like those seen in the 2008 financial meltdown.

Because they feel their knowledge of long-term investing is limited, they decide to seek the assistance of a fee-only financial planner in assessing their personal risk profile and selecting a portfolio of index mutual funds. They hire a local planner who has a master of science degree in personal financial planning and who is also a chartered financial consultant (ChFC). To better assess their risk profile, the fee-only financial planner has Tyler and Claire complete the Risk Assessment Questionnaire, which they do as follows:

Tyler's and Claire's Risk Assessment Questionnaire Results

Question #1: What is your age?
- A. **35 years or younger**
- B. 36 to 54 years
- C. 55 to 64 years
- D. 65 years or older

Question #2: When do you expect to use the money you are now planning to invest?
- A. **In more than 20 years**
- B. In 11 to 20 years
- C. In 5 to 10 years
- D. In less than 5 years

Question #3: Over what length of time do you expect to spend the money once you begin to withdraw from the investment portfolio?
- A. **More than 20 years**
- B. 11 to 20 years
- C. 5 to 10 years
- D. Less than 5 years

Question #4: How would you describe your future income over the next several years?
- A. **Very reliable**
- B. Reliable
- C. Unreliable
- D. Very unreliable

Question #5: Do you have an emergency fund in place and for how long will it cover your expenses in the event of a job loss?

    A. Yes, more than 2 years
    B. **Yes, 6 months to 2 years**
    C. Yes, less than 6 months
    D. No, I do not have an emergency fund

Question #6: How would you describe your level of debt?

    A. I do not have debt
    B. I have a small amount of debt
    C. **I have a fair amount of debt**
    D. I have a significant amount of debt

Question #7: How would you describe your understanding of investments?

    A. Excellent
    B. Good
    C. **Limited**
    D. Extremely limited

Question #8: How many years of experience do you have with investment products?

    A. More than 20 years
    B. 11 to 20 years
    C. 5 to 10 years
    D. **Less than 5 years**

Question #9: In the past, when you have experienced a surprising change in your life that presented challenges, such as losing a job or being forced to relocate, were you:

A. Excited about a new opportunity
B. Concerned about the change, but able to manage the situation
C. **Initially unhappy but eventually able to cope**
D. Extremely unhappy and emotionally stressed

Question #10: If you are a contestant on a game show and have the choice of keeping $10,000 or winning more, which do you choose?

A. A 10% chance of winning $100,000
B. A 25% chance of winning $50,000
C. A 50% chance of winning $20,000
D. **The $10,000**

Question #11: Which investment portfolio would you choose?

A. Portfolio A: Earns either a 50% return or a 25% loss
B. Portfolio B: Earns either a 30% return or a 15% loss
C. Portfolio C: Earns either a 15% return or a 7% loss
D. **Portfolio D: Earns either an 8% return or a 3% loss**

Question #12: If your investment portfolio lost 30% of its value in two months, how long would you wait for your investment portfolio to regain its value?

A. 2 years or more
B. More than 1 year but less than 2 years
C. 6 months to a 1 year
D. **Less than 6 months**

Question #13: Which investment portfolio would you prefer?

    A. Portfolio A: 10% return with a high degree of volatility to principal

    B. Portfolio B: 7% return with a medium degree of volatility to principal

    C. **Portfolio C: 5% return with a low degree of volatility to principal**

    D. Portfolio D: 3% return with no volatility to principal

Question #14: If there was a severe economic crisis and the value of your investment portfolio decreased by 50%, what would you do?

    A. Leave the investment portfolio as is and continue making additional investments as planned

    B. Leave the investment portfolio as is but stop making additional investments

    C. Move a portion of the investment portfolio from more risky stock index mutual funds to less risky bond index mutual funds

    D. **Move the investment portfolio into a federally insured, bank savings account**

Question #15: What is the maximum loss in your investment portfolio that you would be comfortable with over a 6-month period?

    A. 40% to 50% decline

    B. 25% to 30% decline

    C. 10% to 15% decline

    D. **0% to 5% decline**

After completing the questionnaire, Tyler and Claire determine their score by giving themselves four points for the questions they answered with A, three points for questions they answered with B, two points for questions they answered with C, and one point for questions they answered with D. They determine their score is 33 points which classifies Tyler and Claire as moderate risk-takers, on the cusp of being conservative risk-takers. Tyler and Claire deem the results of the questionnaire to be reasonable and in line with how they view themselves and their willingness to take some risk with their long-term investment portfolio.

After completing the Risk Assessment Questionnaire, the next step is to select an asset allocation for their investment portfolio. Before doing so, Tyler and Claire evaluate the various asset allocation models and discuss their personal feelings about financial risk with the help of their fee-only financial planner. They look at the targeted, average, annual, rates of return and, most importantly, the volatility associated with each asset allocation model. After much discussion, they decide to select the Conservative Asset Allocation, Model D, which is not the asset allocation suggested by the Risk Assessment Questionnaire but the one with a level of volatility they are most comfortable.

MODEL D – Conservative Asset Allocation Model:

- % Stock Index Mutual Funds: 40%
- % Bonds Index Mutual Funds: 60%
- Targeted Average Annual Rate of Return: +7.5%

- Targeted High Annual Rate of Return: +25%
- Targeted Low Annual Rate of Return: -20%

Now that Tyler and Claire have decided upon an asset allocation model, they are ready to choose a portfolio of index mutual funds. As conservative investors with a desired asset allocation of 40% stocks and 60% bonds, Tyler and Claire choose Portfolio Type #4, a portfolio for conservative, long-term investors. They see they have a choice between the Simple Portfolio Approach and the Focused Portfolio Approach. The Focused Portfolio Approach includes six different index mutual funds whereas the Simple Portfolio Approach only utilizes two different index mutual funds. Because index mutual funds typically have a minimum initial investment, the Focused Portfolio Approach would require a substantially higher initial investment. As a result, and on the advice of their fee-only financial planner, Tyler and Claire decide to go with the Simple Portfolio Approach and select the following index mutual funds:

PORTFOLIO TYPE #4 – Simple Portfolio Approach for Conservative Investors:

- 40% in the U.S. total stock index mutual fund
- 60% in the U.S. total bond index mutual fund

Now that they have decided on which index mutual funds they will invest in, Tyler and Claire need to select a mutual fund family. Their fee-only financial planner suggests two mutual fund families that have been in business for many years. Claire decides to call each of them and ask questions about their index mutual funds to evaluate the customer service they provide. One of them seems to be better than the other and offers phone service on weekday evenings which fits nicely into Tyler's and Claire's schedules. The mutual fund family also has an excellent reputation for no-load, index mutual funds and for keeping fund expenses to a minimum. The average expense ratio for their index mutual funds is a very low 0.1%. Tyler and Claire also find the website for the mutual fund family to be extremely user-friendly. It provides in-depth analysis of each index mutual fund and also includes tutorials on investing long-term with mutual funds.

Tyler and Claire are comfortable investing $350 per week in their index mutual funds on an ongoing basis after making an initial investment of $3,000 in each fund. They set up an automatic investment plan with the mutual fund family and their bank checking account. They decide to dollar cost average into the two index mutual funds as follows:

- $140 (40% of $350) per week in the U.S. total stock index mutual fund

- $210 (60% of $350) per week in the U.S. total bond index mutual fund

With their index mutual funds selected and having reviewed the prospectus for each, Tyler and Claire just need to select a cost basis methodology. After evaluating the cost basis choices, they choose the average cost methodology for each index mutual fund. With the average cost methodology, each share within each index mutual fund will have the same cost basis and their mutual fund family will be able to provide all necessary record keeping. Tyler and Claire feel the other two methodologies require too much record keeping and they do not perceive any advantage from which they would benefit.

Tyler and Claire are very satisfied with their index mutual fund selections and their long-term investment plan. They anticipate investing for 30 years. The expected annual average rate of return for their conservative investor asset allocation and conservative investment portfolio is 7.5%.

If Tyler and Claire initially invest the minimum requirement of $3,000 to each of their two index mutual funds, for a total initial investment of $6,000, and continue to contribute $350 per week to their portfolio over 30 years, and they earn an average annualized rate of return of 7.4% on their investments (7.5% earned by their investment portfolio less 0.1% for expenses charged by the mutual fund), they will grow their money to $2,069,795 at the end of 30 years.

Note: The accumulated value assumes income taxes due on dividends and capital gain distributions are paid annually out of pocket, outside of the investment portfolio.

PART FOUR

Protect Your Wealth

CHAPTER EIGHTEEN

Establish an Emergency Fund

A critical component in protecting the value of your accumulated investment portfolio is an emergency fund. An emergency fund is important in times of breaks in your employment. Economies have up cycles and down cycles, good times and bad times. During down cycles, recessions often ensue and jobs can be lost. When you lose your job, you will need to draw on personal funds to pay the mortgage, the car payment, health care bills, utility bills, and groceries. It is during these times that the value of your index mutual funds is typically at a low point and the worst time for you to sell shares. It is never a good idea to sell low, after all.

To ensure that you don't have to sell shares of your mutual funds to pay for living expenses during a period of unemployment, it is essential to have an emergency fund in place. The emergency fund should have enough money to cover at least 12 months, and preferably 24 months, of essential living expenses. Essential living expenses being costs that must be paid, expenses that you cannot avoid.

Twelve to twenty-four months may sound like an extended length of time to cover essential living expenses. It is important to realize that some recessions can be lengthy, however, and finding a new job in your field can be an extended process. Having an emergency fund in place will afford you the time you may need to find a position in your field and one that you enjoy. Without an adequate emergency fund, you might be forced to take a position that is not your preference.

After determining how much money you should keep in an emergency fund, you need to determine where to keep it. Your emergency fund should be kept in a secure, federally-backed account that you can access when you need to. There are three best options for your emergency fund:

- a bank or credit union savings account
- a bank or credit union checking account
- United States Treasury bills

All three of these options are backed by the US government. Bank and credit union savings and checking accounts are insured by the FDIC (Federal Deposit Insurance Corporation). The FDIC is an independent federal agency backed by the US government. It insures up to $250,000 per depositor, per insured bank for each ownership category. A married couple, for example, can safeguard up to $1,000,000 by maintaining $250,000 in an account owned by the first spouse, $250,000 in an account owned by the second spouse, and $500,000 in an account owned jointly by the spouses. United States Treasury bills have maturities of less than 30 days. They are also backed by the full faith and credit of the United States government and provide the liquidity you would need during a period of unemployment.

Once you have established your emergency fund, leave it for the time when you may be out of work and without a steady paycheck. A day you hope does not come but one you will be well prepared for in the event it does.

CHAPTER NINETEEN

Insure against Financial Risks

An important component of achieving financial security is managing your financial risk. Financial risk comes in many forms. There is the risk that you die too soon, leaving your loved ones without the means to pay the home mortgage, the car payment, or college tuition. There is the risk that you become disabled and unable to work and earn a living. If you own a home, there is the risk that your home burns down, is flooded, or is damaged in a wind storm. If you own a car, there is the risk that your car will get damaged in an accident or that you cause damage to another car or individual's property or injure another person. There is the risk that you may be sued for injury to another person or libel. Last but not least is the risk of getting sick and needing health care or long-term care in a nursing home or assisted living facility. All of these risks can happen to anyone at any time. As a result, it is important to protect your financial security by managing these risks.

The most practical way to protect yourself from financial risk is to purchase insurance from a highly-rated insurance company. Insurance companies are rated by agencies such as A.M. Best, S&P, and Moody's. You should purchase insurance from a company that achieves strong credit ratings.

- A. M. Best: Superior – A++ or A+; Excellent – A or A-
- S&P: Superior – AAA; Very Strong – AA
- Moody's: Highest Quality – Aaa; High Quality- Aa

Also, when purchasing insurance, utilize an insurance broker. A broker will provide you with quotes from multiple insurance companies and get you the best deal. If you work directly with a company's insurance agent, he or she will only sell you policies from his or her insurance company, which may not offer you the policy that is best and/or least expensive for you.

Following is a list of insurance policies that you should purchase to manage your financial risks:

Term Life Insurance: Term life insurance will protect you and your family in the event of premature death. The term period selected should be long enough to cover the period for which you need to provide financial security for your family. The amount of term life insurance should be sufficient to pay the costs of a funeral and ongoing support of your family's home life and future education costs. Buy an individual term life policy rather than a group policy through your employer. If you purchase a group policy through your employer and subsequently lose your job, you will lose your life insurance coverage as well and may find yourself uninsurable and unable to purchase affordable coverage.

Disability Insurance: Disability insurance will protect you and your family from financial hardship in the event you become disabled and cannot work. The odds of becoming disabled are higher than you would think. It is projected by the Social Security Administration that a twenty-year-old has a one in four chance of becoming disabled before attaining retirement age.

Buy an individual disability insurance policy rather than a group policy through your employer. Employer-provided group disability policies often use a definition of disability that is very restrictive and may not provide a benefit when you need it. Also, a group policy can be canceled by the employer at any time. And if you were to leave your employer, you would also lose your coverage.

When purchasing a disability insurance policy, look for a policy that is both non-cancelable and guaranteed renewable. This will ensure that the premium and benefits cannot be changed and that the policy cannot be canceled unless you fail to pay your premium. Some policies are only guaranteed renewable. This type of policy, however, offers you no guarantee against future premium increases. You should also look for a policy with an inflation protection option that allows you to increase your coverage in the future. Policies should also provide benefits until you reach retirement age rather than for a limited three-year or five-year period. Last, benefit payments should have a cost-of-living adjustment so that payments keep pace with inflation and rising living expenses.

Long-Term Care Insurance: Approximately 60 percent of people will require some form of long-term care support over their lifetimes. Long-term care is extremely expensive, whether it is provided in a nursing home, assisted living facility, or administered in the home environment by a home health aide. Health insurance and Medicare do not cover long-term care. So unless you are very wealthy and can afford to pay for care yourself or if you are very poor and qualify for Medicaid, it is important to purchase long-term care insurance.

When purchasing a long-term care policy, look for a policy that provides a daily benefit equal to the average daily costs associated with your geographic area. The policy should also contain an inflation protection benefit to ensure that it will provide a benefit that is adequate in the future. The policy should also provide at least three years of care coverage and preferably five to six years of care coverage.

Most policies will offer a waiting period, which is the amount of time you will have to cover costs out of your own pocket before the insurance policy will provide a benefit. The longer the waiting period in place, the lower the insurance policy premium. A ninety-day waiting period is typical on most policies.

Last, most people would prefer to receive care in their own homes. Make sure the policy you purchase provides for adult day care or for a home health aide to assist you. Some policies may also cover the cost of making adjustments to the home to make living in the home easier.

Homeowner's Insurance: Your home is likely the most expensive asset you will ever own and as such needs to be protected against damage and loss. The typical homeowner's policy will cover the primary dwelling and other detached structures on the property, such as a detached garage, personal property, and living expenses incurred due to loss of use.

Coverage on the dwelling and other buildings is on a replacement-cost basis without deduction for depreciation as long as, at the time of loss, the amount of insurance on the dwelling is at least 80 percent of the full replacement cost of the dwelling. Therefore, it is very important to know what the replacement cost of your home is for your given market. If the replacement cost of your home given the cost of supplies and labor is $300,000, then the home should be insured for at least $240,000.

Personal property loss is typically covered on a cash-value basis, meaning the loss will be paid on the market value of the property as of the date of loss but not greater than the amount required to repair or replace. It can be covered on a replacement-cost basis but at a much higher premium. Personal property is generally insured as a percentage of the amount of insurance on the dwelling. Although the percentage varies by the individual insurance contract form, most policies will provide coverage on personal property equal to 60 percent of the amount of coverage on the dwelling. Thus, if your dwelling is insured for $240,000, then the personal property will likely be insured up to $144,000. It is important to realize, however, that the homeowner's policy will place limits on specified types of personal property. For example, coverage on jewelry loss due to theft is typically only covered up to $1,500. Coverage on silverware due to theft is typically covered up to $2,500, while computer equipment is typically covered up to $4,000. Other such limitations on personal property will be detailed in your specific policy form.

Similar to coverage on personal property, the coverage provided for additional living expenses incurred while the home is uninhabitable and being repaired is a percentage of the amount of insurance on the dwelling. Typically, it is 30 percent of the insurance on the dwelling, but it can vary depending on the specific policy form.

Last, a homeowner's policy will provide the insured with personal liability coverage and medical payments to others. The standard limit on personal liability coverage is $100,000 per occurrence and $1,000 on medical payments to others. These limits may be increased.

Events like floods, earthquakes, and mold infestation are typically not covered by the basic homeowner's policy. To be insured against these perils, you will typically need to purchase a rider to your base policy at an additional cost.

Renters Insurance: If you rent an apartment or house, you should purchase renters insurance. Renters insurance will cover the full replacement cost of your belongings in the event of loss due to fire, lightning, windstorm, hail, water damage, and theft. Renters insurance is extremely inexpensive and well worth the minor cost.

Auto Insurance: If you own a car, then auto insurance is a must. As an owner of an auto, you are subject to multiple types of risk including damage to or loss of your car, legal liability for damages you may cause to others as well as physical injury to yourself, members of your family, and others.

To protect yourself from these risks, auto insurance will provide you with liability coverage, medical payments coverage, uninsured motorist coverage, and physical damage coverage. When purchasing auto insurance coverage, you should purchase as much coverage as you can afford. The more coverage you purchase, the higher the premium. In addition to choosing coverage amounts, you will need to select a deductible. The higher the deductible you choose, the lower your premium will be. You should choose as high a deductible as you can comfortably afford to pay in the event of a claim. When purchasing auto insurance, obtain quotes from multiple carriers as prices between insurers can vary greatly.

Umbrella Insurance: We live in a very litigious society. You can be personally sued if someone trips on your sidewalk and injures himself or herself or if you injure someone on the golf course with an errant drive shot. The liability coverage provided by a typical homeowner's policy or auto policy does not provide sufficient levels of liability coverage in the event you are sued. Therefore, it is important to have additional liability protection through an umbrella liability policy.

An umbrella policy will provide coverage over and beyond the liability coverage provided by your homeowner's and automobile policies. A typical umbrella policy will provide $1 million of liability coverage but can provide coverage up to $5 million. You should purchase umbrella coverage sufficient to protect the value of your assets. Most insurers will require you to also obtain your homeowner's and automobile policy through them before they issue you an umbrella policy and will typically require that the homeowner's and automobile policies provide up to $500,000 of liability coverage. Requirements will vary from insurer to insurer.

Umbrella liability coverage is generally not that expensive, typically, only a few hundred dollars per year. Given the litigious nature of our society, however, it is coverage well worth purchasing.

Health Insurance: No matter their age or current health, anyone can get sick or injured and require medical care. A 20-year-old can get sick, be diagnosed with cancer, or be injured on a bicycle ride or hike. That being the case, everyone of all ages, should carry health insurance.

If your employer does not offer you health insurance and you do not qualify for government-provided health insurance such as Medicaid, you will need to purchase a private health insurance policy. Individuals and families can purchase affordable health insurance coverage in competitive health insurance marketplaces as a result of the Patient Protection and Affordable Care Act signed into law in 2010. Commonly referred to as Obamacare, these health insurance marketplaces provide information on health coverage options and help you evaluate and compare private health insurance policies. Health insurance policies offered in these marketplaces meet specific benefits and cost standards and provide excellent coverage.

Depending upon your family size and level of income, you may be eligible for a subsidy which will offset the cost of the health insurance policies that are offered. You are able to see the amount of the subsidy you are eligible for at the time you submit your application for coverage. The subsidy is applied to the premium at the time it is due.

The federal health insurance marketplace website can be accessed at www.healthcare.gov. Some states have their own health insurance marketplace website. If your state has its own, www.healthcare.gov will direct you to it.

Identity Theft Insurance: It is important to protect yourself from identity theft. Identity theft occurs when a criminal steals your personally identifiable information such as your name, date of birth, address, driver's license number, and social security number, and uses the information for their financial gain. As a victim of identity theft, you can be subject to fraudulent charges and damages to your credit history. Recovering from identity theft can be an expensive and onerous process.

Identity theft insurance covers you for losses related to the reporting and recovery process. Most policies will cover such things as legal fees for court hearings and lawyers; fees for the replacement of stolen documents such as driver's licenses and social security cards; lost wages; fees charged by a financial institution as a result of the theft; and the cost to place fraud alerts on your accounts. Identity theft insurance will not cover direct monetary losses resulting from fraudulent charges and unauthorized use of your credit accounts. Many companies will monitor your credit and provide $1 million in coverage for eligible expenses for a modest premium.

CHAPTER TWENTY

Important and Necessary Documents

Although no one likes to think about becoming incapacitated or dying, it is extremely important to plan for these events. The planning and steps you take in advance regarding these events will make things easier for your loved ones and ensure that your wishes are carried out. There are a number of documents that are important and necessary to help protect your wealth, legacy, and personal wishes.

Last Will and Testament: It is very important to write a last will and testament. The last will and testament should state who should be your personal representative, otherwise known as your executor, who the beneficiaries are, and what assets your beneficiaries will receive. If you have children who are minors, your last will and testament should state who will be the guardian of your children.

The last will and testament should also state how potential estate taxes will be paid and by whom. For example, you may decide that only beneficiaries receiving property outside of specific bequests bear the estate tax burden. It can also state that beneficiaries of property distributed outside the terms of the last will and testament, such as an annuity death benefit, pay a proportionate share of the estate tax.

Assets distributed through the terms of the last will and testament are administered through the probate process. Probate is a court-administered process through which the assets of the estate are retitled to the heirs. Depending on the size and complexity of the estate, the probate process can take from six months to many years to complete. Many assets can be distributed outside the terms of the last will and testament, however, and subsequently, outside of the probate process. By naming beneficiaries on such assets as mutual funds, life insurance policies, and annuity contracts, ownership of such assets will pass directly to the named beneficiaries as of the date of death by the terms of the contract. The beneficiaries will need to complete a beneficiary claim form and provide a copy of the death certificate to receive their assets. When assets are transferred through a beneficiary designation, proceeds will likely be received much more quickly than proceeds received through the probate process. It is strongly suggested to transfer assets via a beneficiary designation if at all possible due to the ease and quickness of the process.

Letter of Instruction: In addition to writing a last will and testament, you should also write a letter of instruction for your personal representative. The letter of instruction should provide the information your personal representative will need to arrange your funeral and settle your estate. You should provide instructions on the funeral home and service you desire, the newspapers in which you wish your obituary to be printed, whether to be buried or cremated, the cemetery in which you wish to be buried, the location of any cemetery deed you may own, and any wishes you might have for a grave marker or stone inscription.

The letter of instruction should also include a summary of your financial assets, including bank accounts, investment accounts, stocks, bonds, annuity contracts, life insurance contracts, real estate, and automobiles. The summary should include the location of all related documents including the deed(s) to your home(s) and title(s) to your automobile(s). The locations of a secured fireproof box and safe deposit box and the location of their keys should also be provided.

Personal Property Memorandum: You should also write a personal property memorandum detailing specifically who should receive which pieces of your tangible personal property. This will assist in ensuring that your property is distributed as you would wish and make the process easier for everyone involved. Just because your beneficiaries get along while you are alive does not mean they will be able to amicably divide your personal property without your guidance. Save undue hardship among your beneficiaries by deciding for them who should get the crystal, the photographs, the silverware, and various pieces of jewelry. The more specific you are with instructions for your personal representative and your beneficiaries, the easier it will be for all involved in the distribution of your assets and the settling of your estate.

Durable General Power of Attorney: Unfortunately, it is not uncommon for people to become incapacitated during their lifetimes and thus, it is important to plan for the possibility and ensure that certain documents are in place. One such document is the durable general power of attorney. The durable general power of attorney will enable you to name a person who can make all financial decisions on your behalf in the event you become incapacitated and unable to do so yourself. The person you name should be someone you trust explicitly and who is reliable and organized.

Durable Medical Power of Attorney: A durable medical power of attorney will enable you to name a person to make medical decisions on your behalf in the event you are unable to do so. If you are unconscious, the person you name to represent you will be able to discuss your medical condition with your doctors and make decisions related to your care. It should be noted that some states do not recognize a durable medical power of attorney for life-and-death decisions. In such states, an additional document, a living will declaration is required and will enable the person named in the declaration to make the decision as to when life support should be terminated when there is no reasonable expectation for recovery.

HIPAA Authorization: Last, a HIPAA Authorization and waiver form should be completed. The form will allow the person named as your representative in the durable medical power of attorney to access your health information records. Without this signed form, it may be difficult for your representative to access the information he or she needs to make informed decisions on your behalf.

It is very important that you discuss with your personal representative your wishes and his or her very important role in making decisions on your behalf. Your personal representative should be given signed originals of these critical documents. You should also name your personal representative on your safe deposit box so that they will be able to access the box when necessary.

CHAPTER TWENTY-ONE

Perform an Annual Checkup

Once per year, you should perform an annual checkup on your personal finances. Whether it is timed with the start of the new calendar year, the filing of your income tax return, or your birthday, it is very important that a review be done on an annual basis. Doing so will ensure that your personal finances are on track and that the previous decisions related to your personal finances are still valid.

The following items should be included in your annual checkup:

- Track your spending and make necessary adjustments to your spending habits to ensure that you are saving and investing to grow your money adequately.

- Verify that your emergency fund is adequate for at least one year's worth of essential living expenses.

- Verify that your current asset allocation is within 5 percent of your desired asset allocation. This should be done for all investment accounts, including your 401(k), IRA, and other personal investment accounts.

- Perform a credit check with the three credit bureaus—Equifax, Experian, and TransUnion—to ensure your credit score is excellent and the information on file for you is accurate. If any of the credit bureaus have information that is inaccurate, file a dispute with them. Disputes can be filed online and are generally resolved without issue once supporting documentation is forwarded to them.

- Reevaluate your insurance protection needs for life, disability, long-term care, home, auto, umbrella, health, and identity theft. Verify that your current levels of protection are adequate.

- Review and update, if necessary, your last will and testament, letter of instruction, and personal property memorandum.

- Review all beneficiary designations for any life insurance policy, mutual fund, annuity contract, and other assets for which you have designated beneficiaries. Update the designations for any changes, including name changes and address changes.

- Review and update, if necessary, all documents related to your support during periods of incapacity, including the durable general power of attorney, durable medical power of attorney, the living will declaration, and your HIPAA authorization and waiver form. Provide signed originals of updated documents to your personal representative.

Once you have completed your personal finance annual checkup, ensure that all documents are safely filed away, preferably in a secured fireproof box or safe deposit box.

Conclusion

I hope you have found *Grow Your Money Protect Your Wealth* to be informative and helpful, and now are encouraged to begin a long-term investment plan for yourself. With some planning and effort, you will be able to grow your money and protect your wealth. With focus and determination, you can build a life in retirement that is financially secure for you and your family.

Please remember, know yourself. Understand and appreciate your own level of risk tolerance and choose an asset allocation and investment portfolio you can live with through volatile economic times. To thy own self be true and invest, invest, invest—through market ups and market downs.

Grow your money, protect your wealth, and enjoy the freedom of living a life in retirement with financial security.

All the best,
Matthew Mellett, MS, CLU, ChFC

Notes

CHAPTER THREE:
How Do Index Mutual Funds Grow Your Money

As an example, let us look at a sample of historical values of the S&P 500 index.

"S&P 500 Index – 90 Year Historical Chart," Macrotrends.net, accessed May 20, 2024, http://www.macrotrends.net/2324/sp-500-historical-chart-data.

CHAPTER EIGHT:
Select Your Asset Allocation

A study by Brinson, Hood, and Beebower

Gary P. Brinson, L. Randolph Hood, and Gilbert L. Beebower, "Determinants of Portfolio Performance," *Financial Analysts Journal*, July – August 1986.

CHAPTER THIRTEEN:
Tax-Advantaged Personal Investment Plans

RMDs must commence by age seventy-three if you were born between 1951 and 1959, and by age seventy-five if you were born in 1960 and later.

"401k Withdrawal Rules: What You Need to Know," Investopedia.com, accessed March 19, 2024, http://www.investopedia.com/articles/personal-finance/111615/how-401k-works-after-retirement.asp.

CHAPTER NINETEEN:
Insure Against Financial Risks

It is projected by the Social Security Administration that a twenty-year-old has a one in four chance of becoming disabled before attaining retirement age.

"Understanding Social Security Disability Benefits," Social Security Matters, accessed February 9, 2024, https://blog.ssa.gov/understanding-social-security-disability-benefits.

Approximately 60 percent of people will require some form of long-term care support over their lifetimes.

"What is Long-Term Care (LTC) and Who Needs it," LongTermCare.gov, accessed February 9, 2024, http://www.acl.gov/ltc.

*"He that waits upon fortune
is never sure of a dinner."*

—Benjamin Franklin

READER NOTES

READER NOTES

READER NOTES

READER NOTES

www.ingramcontent.com/pod-product-compliance
Lightning Source LLC
LaVergne TN
LVHW021825060526
838201LV00058B/3516